Still Fulfilled

A Christian Faith Journey through the

Heartache of Infertility,

the Hope of Adoption

and God's Healing Grace

ANNE TEAGARDEN

Publish Authority

Editor: Janet Silburn
Cover Design: Raeghan Rebstock
Interior Design: Teresa Evans

ISBN 978-1-967213-17-7 (Paperback)
ISBN 978-1-967213-18-4 (eBook)

Published 2026 by Publish Authority,
www.publishauthority.com

Printed in the United States of America

To my husband who walked this hard road with me.

*To all the hurting women who don't see a way out of your pain –
yet – this book is for you.*

Contents

I see you.
    I hear you.
    I know your pain.
    Let me carry it for you.
    ~ JESUS

First, I want to say that I'm so sorry for what you are going through. If you are reading this book, most likely your heart is breaking. I've been there. I know the feeling of empty arms. I know you may not want to read this book. All you really want is to get pregnant and move on, or to move on and forget about trying to get pregnant. Perhaps you are long past this and don't want to dredge up those feelings again. I get it.

Would it surprise you to learn that I didn't want to write this book for many of the same reasons? Taking out our pain and looking it in the eye to deal with it is never fun. But I would daresay it is necessary for healing and wholeness. Pain stuffed does not go away. Even getting pregnant or adopting will not fully heal the pain of what you have already suffered and may still be suffering.

Rest assured, God has not forgotten you. He longs to hold you in his arms and speak words of comfort to you. I hope to teach you how to listen.

Like many of us, as a little girl I always dreamed of being a mom. I used to go around the house with a couch pillow under my shirt, pretending to be pregnant. I wanted to have five children – three by birth and two adopted.

Fast forward – after four years of marriage, we decided it was time to start a family. I assumed I would conceive right away. I was surprised when I didn't. Of course, everyone said, "Give it time."

I gave it time. That was twenty-eight years ago. I never conceived. I'm ten years past my last period. I have no Cinderella story to share.

What I do have is understanding of the heartache you may be going through. Some of you reading this will get pregnant with or without help. Some won't. God will meet each of you where you are and carry you through. Even in this, God is working all things together for good. He wastes nothing.

I know we would all love to have the fairy book ending. But this book is not about your womb; it is about your heart. It's about understanding the pain in your heart and giving it to the one who loves you most. It's about laying the anger on the altar and exchanging it for His peace and goodness. To find freedom, I had to shift my focus from the gift to the giver Himself. It's a different kind of grace. It's knowing that the one who made me loves me more than I can imagine, whether my prayer is answered as I would like, or not.

As you read on, you will see that my story has a happy ending. It includes the blessing of my two amazing, adopted children. I got to be a mom! More importantly, my heart has no bitterness, and I can love them fully. This is my story of moving beyond barrenness and bitterness to beautiful abundance. You can have a happy ending, too. You can be still fulfilled.

My prayer for you is that by the end of this book, you will feel understood and will begin to find freedom and healing. I wrote this for you.

Now, take my hand, and let's start this journey toward wholeness and healing. I've walked this road before you. I know the Way.

Jesus answered, 'I am the way, the truth and the life.'
John 14:6

CHAPTER 1

You Are Not Alone

Now Sarai was childless because she was not able to conceive.
Genesis 11:30

The dry leaves swept across the barren ground with a hot wind that dried my tears. It was an apt picture of how I was feeling – barren. Two years of marriage to Abram, a fine man, and yet I have given him nothing. Nothing. The other women are beginning to whisper. I know what they're saying, because I'm thinking it, too. "Sarai must have sinned and Yahweh is punishing her." "Poor Abram. He should have chosen a different wife."

What have I done, Lord, to deserve this shame? I serve my husband as a wife should. All my life, I have tried to live honorably. I don't understand what is happening – or rather not happening to me. What could be the reason for this? Abram is a righteous man. I know you are not punishing him. He loves you and serves you.

Have you heard our prayers for a baby? Are you listening?

~

So many times have I questioned Yahweh this way. Is he listening? My friends are all having babies, and they look at me with pity and shame. I'm always the last to know of their expected joy. Why me? Why not them?

I've often identified with the story of Sarah and Abraham from the Bible (named Sarai and Abram before God changed their names). One morning, as I was reflecting on infertility, the first paragraph above came to me from the Holy Spirit. It was like I was in Sarah's head. It was thousands of years ago, but she felt just like me.

As women, we identify with Sarah's anguish. We understand her shame and embarrassment, her longing and the cry of her heart. We ask questions like the ones above. We probably even understand her desperate measures in giving her servant Hagar to Abraham to have a baby for her.

Somehow, it was a comfort to me to know that I was not the first woman to struggle with infertility. Remember Hannah?

In her deep anguish Hannah prayed to the LORD, *weeping bitterly. And she made a vow, saying, "*LORD *Almighty, if you will only look on your servant's misery and remember me, and not forget your servant but give her a son, then I will give him to the* LORD *for all the days of his life, and no razor will ever be used on his head."*

As she kept on praying to the LORD, *Eli observed her mouth. Hannah was praying in her heart, and her lips were moving but her voice was not heard. Eli thought she was drunk and said to her, "How long are you going to stay drunk? Put away your wine."*

"Not so, my lord," Hannah replied, "I am a woman who is deeply troubled. I have not been drinking wine or beer; I was pouring out my soul to the LORD. Do not take your servant for a wicked woman; I have been praying here out of my great anguish and grief." 1 Samuel 1:10-16

Thousands of years ago, a woman struggling to get pregnant felt just like me and you. She felt "great anguish and grief." Can you identify?

You are not alone.

Sarah, Hannah, Rachel, Elizabeth, all Biblical women who cried out to God for a baby. There is even the barren Shunamite woman who had given up asking, but God gave her a baby anyway (See II Kings, Chapter 4). What has been hard for me is this - where in the Bible is the story of the barren woman who did not get pregnant? I haven't found it. I'm sure there were some, like the Shunamite, but we don't hear of them. However, I know plenty of God-fearing, God-loving women who are like me. It never happened for them, or at least it hasn't yet.

We all have questions. Some I will help you answer. Some, God will help you answer. Some will never be answered, and you will need to learn to be content with that. Don't think for a minute that God is punishing you. I'm sure that's what these Old Testament women were told. Jesus paid the price for all our sins. God knows your anguish and has compassion for you, not condemnation. Remember, you are not alone.

PRAYER:

Father, my heart still longs to get pregnant and give birth to a baby. I know you put this desire in my heart. Thank you for walking with me during this difficult season. Sometimes I feel like I can't breathe, I'm so fearful and stressed. Other times, I can't stop crying. There are times when I feel numb and times when I feel at peace. This is so hard. Like Sarah and Hannah, I will pour out my anguish before you. Take my feelings of sadness and confusion and bring peace and clarity. Let the peace of Christ rule in my heart.

REFLECTION:

Lord, here are my unanswered questions...

____

____

____

____

____

If you have accepted Jesus as your Savior and surrendered your life to Him, remember that He loves you and lives in you. If you haven't yet, know that He loves you, as well! If that's you, take a moment and ask Him to make Himself known to you. Yield your future to Him and His plans. I guarantee it's the best thing you will ever do! I can honestly say that I would not have wanted to travel this journey without the awareness of how much Jesus loves me and is with me.

CHAPTER 2

Grieving the Losses

Those who sow with tears,
Will reap with songs of joy.
Those who go out weeping, carrying seeds to sow
Will return with songs of joy, carrying sheaves with them.
Psalm 126:5-6

When a woman has a miscarriage, she grieves. She grieves never getting to know that child or holding "the baby" in her arms. There is obvious loss and people understand that.

With infertility, the loss is less obvious. But I experienced loss nonetheless. So much loss. I didn't know how to process what I was grieving exactly, much less how to grieve it. One day, I read something in a book that helped me define it. (I wish I remembered what book it was.)

It described the losses something like this. First, you lose the joy of immediate gratification and surprise at being pregnant. Then you lose the spontaneity of intimacy with your spouse. It is replaced with "We have to do it tonight! I'm ovulating!" You lose control of deciding when you want to get pregnant. (Though control is an illusion for all of us.) Then you lose being "normal". Then you lose the privacy of it as you receive medical help.

Sometimes, you lose the biological connection if there is a sperm donor, or egg donor, or adoption. Sometimes you lose the experience of pregnancy, childbirth, and breastfeeding. Each of these losses needs to be acknowledged and grieved. They are truly losses.

Grieving the loss of a biological child is so important. Even if your womb is opened at some point and you have the joy of bearing a child, you still need to grieve the loss of the child that you would have had when you first started trying. Getting pregnant at twenty-seven is totally different than getting pregnant at thirty-seven.

For many years, I tracked how old my child would be. I would think, "If I had gotten pregnant right away, that child would be two now." I would look around at two-year-old children and imagine having one. I thought about how old I would have been when they graduated high school. That imaginary child began to take on a life of their own.

I also had a name picked out if it was a girl, "Grace Margaret." My name is Anne, and the meaning of my name is "full of grace." I thought it would be neat to name her the meaning of my name. My middle name is Margaret, and I was named after my mother, who was Margaret Ann. It carried on the tradition while changing it a bit. That name felt so right. It was 1997 when we began trying to get pregnant. Both my sister and sister-in-law became pregnant that year and gave birth four days apart in June of 1998. Obviously, that was hard. Why not me? But the biggest blow came when my sister-in-law named her new baby girl, "Grace." I felt so much anguish. It was like the Heavens had added insult to injury.

About a year later, I decided that part of my healing process would be to make my niece, Grace, a baby album. I knew her mom didn't scrapbook, and since Grace was a third child, like me, I wanted to make sure she got a baby book. It was healing to pour my love into the project as an act of letting go of "my" Grace. I didn't think grandparents should have two grandkids with the same name, so I had to let go of the name and the imaginary child along with it.

At some point, I had a funeral in my mind for my baby Grace. I gave her into God's hands, the same as I would have an actual child. That child of my imagination, born in 1997 or 1998 would never be. This opened the door for new joy and blessing.

God cannot give us a new blessing while we are holding onto something from the past. Our hands are full. We are stuck in that place. In order to move on, we must let go of demanding *our* will. We have to let go of the past. We have to let go of the longed-for biological child born at a certain time in our lives. Free up your love for another child or person that God wants to bring into your life.

Holding on to the past and to our own demands will *always* lead to bitterness. Holding on to self-pity will *always* lead to bitterness. Holding on to anger and frustration will *always* lead to bitterness. Unfortunately, bitterness blocks joy and healing. Bitterness is internally corrosive. It leads to death. It will never be life-giving.

So – it's a choice. Choose to let go of these things and choose life. Think of it as choosing between the light and the dark.

In the year 2000, I had lunch with a young woman in our

church. She and her husband were going to start a family soon, and she was afraid of not getting pregnant. She wanted to talk with me about her fears. She complimented me on how impressed she was that I could talk about it freely and not be bitter. I remember her saying, "If it were me, I would be so hurt and angry. I don't think I could handle it like you are. You're such an inspiration."

I chuckled and thanked her for the compliment. The work that God had wrought was visible to others. I was, however, completely honest with her. She didn't know me two years ago when I was steeped in hurt, anger, envy, and self-pity. I explained that it had been eating me alive, and I knew I couldn't go on like that. I chose to accept God's will over my own, and I worked to grieve my loss. I think that impressed her more. She realized I wasn't superhuman or extra-spiritual. I had felt it, gone through it and come out shining on the other side.

Are you ready to let go and receive what God wants to give you? Open your hands in faith. See what He will do. Trust Him.

Prayer:

Jesus, I am grieving the loss of my dreams, loss of control, loss of a biological baby. You know how much my heart hurts and aches. My arms feel so empty. I feel so broken. Please heal these hurt, broken places inside me. I give you the child in my imagination and let go of her/him. Help me to grieve and move on. Help me get ready to receive what you want to give us. I trust you, that you will bring good out of this heartache." *And we know that in all things God works for the good of those who love him, who have been called according to his purpose."* (Romans 8:28).

REFLECTION:

This is what I am grieving...

____

____

____

____

____

How is my husband processing these losses?

____

____

____

____

____

CHAPTER 3

Surrendering My Plan

Many are the plans in a person's heart,
but it is the LORD's purpose that prevails.
Proverbs 19:21

I love to plan. Shortly after Grant and I married, we decided to make some goals and plans. We talked about long-term goals like buying a house and starting a family. However, when our timeline indicated that it was time to buy a house, we realized we needed to change our plan. As we felt the Lord calling us to minister in urban, non-Christian, high-cost-of-living areas, we surrendered the plan to own a house. We told the Lord we would be content to rent forever if that was what he desired for us. We laid homeownership on the altar and submitted to God's will for us. (Ten years later, He led us to buy a house. Surrendering doesn't always mean it's a "no." Sometimes it's just a different timing.)

Our plan for children was to start a family after five years of marriage. We married young, and that sounded about right to us. So naive! We thought we had total control over these things! Laughable now. When we had been married four years, I told

Grant that I was ready to start a family. He reminded me of our five-year plan. I asked if we could move it up and after much discussion, we decided to wait a few months more, until after we moved to California for him to attend seminary.

I still remember January 1997. Four months before our fifth wedding anniversary, we went for it! Deciding to get pregnant and start a family was one of the most exciting things in my life outside of getting engaged. I was *sure* I would get pregnant right away. I would get pain in my side when I ovulated, so most months I knew when I was ovulating. The night we were intimate during ovulation was so romantic. What I remember most is the excitement over the next few weeks of waiting for the good news. I vividly remember one night when Grant and I went for a walk on campus and stood on "Chapel Hill." There we were, standing in the moonlight. Grant grabbed me and kissed me and looked deep in my eyes. He marveled that even then, I might have our baby inside me. It was the most wonderful, "oneness" feeling. For whatever reason, that moment is forever burned into my memory.

Somehow, when I got my period that month, that moment felt like a fraud. *I* felt like a fraud. Of course, we knew better than to be discouraged that it didn't happen the first month. The second month was just as exciting and anticipatory. Surely it will happen THIS month! I began to buy maternity clothing at the thrift store and dream about being a mom.

Again, my period. Each month, little by little, the excitement and enthusiasm began to give way to anxiety and fear, until there was more anxiety than excitement. Suddenly, all of my romantic notions about getting pregnant came crashing down. I stuffed the maternity clothing under the bed. Grant focused on schoolwork. I stifled my feelings, continually telling myself it would happen - it just takes time.

I remember the inner wrestling match between my flesh

and my faith. I would feel disappointed and anxious but then talk to myself about God's faithfulness. I would continually affirm my trust in Him. I did all right at first, but it wasn't without struggle. This was all part of God's plan, right? That way, when we did conceive, we would know it was God's gift. I was okay with that plan, but hurry up, please.

I am not a person who likes to wait for things. I am a "do it now" sort of person. If something needs to be done, let's do it. I am more tempered in this now, but at that age, I was used to making things happen. If people wanted something done, they came to me because they knew I would make it happen. Now I had to face the fact that I couldn't make this happen. That was new. It was humbling. It was a struggle.

Already, there was loss. That initial spark and excitement were gone. It wasn't going to be something that just happened. It's important to acknowledge this loss. Not everyone will understand the feeling of loss. They comfortingly say, "Just give it more time. It will happen..." But then it doesn't, and there is more loss.

Any trial we go through in life can have one of two outcomes. It can drive us closer to the heart of God and strengthen our relationship with Him; it can allow Him to bring beauty from ashes. Or - we can turn our back on God and let the situation drive us away from God; we can blame Him and choose to no longer trust Him. Not a good plan.

You may be at the crossroads right now. I was tempted to run from God, but time and time again I turned toward Him. And that made all the difference. Turn to Him and seek *His* plan. Then surrender to it.

PRAYER:

Lord, surrendering things to you is hard, especially when they are things I really, really want. You know my desire for a baby. I lay that desire on your altar and ask for Your will to be done. If it is not Your will for us to conceive, please show us what Your will is and help my heart get on board with that. Please help me grapple with this trial and come out stronger on the other side. Comfort me in this loss and disappointment. I love You and trust You.

REFLECTION:

Lord, who do you want to be for me in this trial? (Write down whatever you sense Him saying in your heart. The next chapter explains more about how to do this.)

____

____

____

____

CHAPTER 4

Gentle Whispers

And after the fire came a gentle whisper.
1 Kings 19:12

You may be wondering, "How do I seek God's plan? How do I know what He wants? Could He just text me?" I know that's how I felt. "Just tell me your plan, God! Tell me why this isn't happening!" I would yell at Him. I wish I had known then what I know now. At the time that I was struggling with infertility, I could occasionally sense what God was saying to me but was often unsure.

Then one day, a friend of ours introduced us to life-changing material called "The Four Keys to Hearing God's Voice." We can honestly say that it has been one of the most useful and impactful teachings of our lives. It took a bit of practice to really "tune in," but once we got the hang of it, we realized how much God had to say to us. His voice is so gentle, kind, and wise. Our intimacy with the Lord has grown exponentially through our conversations with Him. Wounds have been healed. Wrong mindsets have been corrected. Insights have been gained. Why had we been listening to the enemy so much more than our loving, heavenly Father all those years prior?

You have likely heard Him speak to you, too, even if you didn't realize it. Jesus desires an intimate relationship with us and is always speaking to us in that *"still, small voice"* (1 Kings 19:11-13). To help you heal along this journey, I have included some reflection questions that require asking God a question and then listening for His answer. If you are not familiar with hearing directly from God, this is your opportunity to learn this very valuable skill. The idea is to be still, picture Jesus with you, ask the question, and write down His answer coming to your heart and mind. This will allow you to get His perspective. I've found His answers are always better than mine. The secret is to listen with your spirit, not your head.

To help you learn this skill, I have included the following article on "The Four Keys to Hearing God's Voice" with Dr. Mark Virkler's permission, based on his book by the same title. This will be helpful to read **before** you start answering the reflection questions. Please, please, please, take the time to learn and practice this skill as it will bring transformation in your life like nothing else. Imagine being able to hear God's loving heart toward you!

How to Hear God's Voice – By Dr. Mark Virkler [1]

She had done it again! Instead of coming straight home from school like she was supposed to, she had gone to her friend's house. Without permission. Without our knowledge. Without doing her chores.

With a ministering household that included remnants of three struggling families plus our own toddler and newborn, my wife simply couldn't handle all the work on her own. Everyone had to pull their own weight. Everyone had age-appropriate tasks they were expected to complete. At fourteen, Rachel and her younger brother were living with us while her parents tried to overcome lifestyle patterns that had resulted in the children running away to escape the dysfunction. I felt sorry for Rachel, but, honestly my wife was my greatest concern.

Now Rachel had ditched her chores to spend time with her friends. It wasn't the first time, but if I had anything to say about it, it would be the last. I intended to lay down the law when she got home and make it very clear that if she was going to live under my roof, she would obey my rules.

But...she wasn't home yet. And I had recently been learning to hear God's voice more clearly. Maybe I should try to see if I could hear anything from Him about the situation. Maybe He could give me a way to get her to do what she was supposed to (i.e. what I wanted her to do). So I went to my office and reviewed what the Lord had been teaching me from Habakkuk 2:1,2: *"I will stand on my guard post and station myself on the rampart; And I will keep watch to see what He will speak to me..."* Then the Lord answered me and said, 'Record the vision....'"

Habakkuk said, "I will stand on my guard post..." (Hab. 2:1). **The first key to hearing God's voice is to go to a quiet place and still our own thoughts and emotions.** Psalm 46:10 encourages us to be still, let go, cease striving, and know that He is God. In Psalm 37:7 we are called to "be still before the Lord and wait patiently for Him." There is a deep inner knowing in our spirits that each of us can experience when we quiet our flesh and our minds. Practicing the art of biblical meditation helps silence the outer noise and distractions clamoring for our attention.

I didn't have a guard post but I did have an office, so I went there to quiet my temper and my mind. Loving God through a quiet worship song is one very effective way to become still. In 2 Kings 3, Elisha needed a word from the Lord so he said, "Bring me a minstrel," and as the minstrel played, the Lord spoke. I have found that playing a worship song on my autoharp is the quickest way for me to come to stillness. I need to choose my song carefully; boisterous songs of praise do not bring me to stillness, but rather gentle songs that express my love and worship. And it isn't enough just to sing the song into the cosmos – I come into the Lord's presence most quickly and easily when I use my godly imagination to see the truth that He is right here with me and I sing my songs to Him, personally.

"I will keep watch to see," said the prophet. To receive the pure word of God, it is very important that my heart be properly focused as I become still, because my focus is the source of the intuitive flow. If I fix my eyes upon Jesus (Heb. 12:2), the intuitive flow comes from Jesus. But if I fix my gaze upon some desire of my heart, the intuitive flow comes out of that desire. To have a pure flow I must become still and carefully fix my eyes upon Jesus. Quietly worshiping the King and receiving out of the stillness that follows quite easily accomplishes this.

So I used **the second key to hearing God's voice: As you pray, fix the eyes of your heart upon Jesus, seeing in the Spirit the dreams and visions of Almighty God.** Habakkuk was actually looking for vision as he prayed. He opened the eyes of his heart, and looked into the spirit world to see what God wanted to show him.

God has always spoken through dreams and visions, and He specifically said that they would come to those upon whom the Holy Spirit is poured out (Acts 2:1-4, 17).

Being a logical, rational person, observable facts that could be verified by my physical senses were the foundations of my life, including my spiritual life. I had never thought of opening the eyes of my heart and looking for vision. However, I have come to believe that this is exactly what God wants me to do. He gave me eyes in my heart to see in the spirit the vision and movement of Almighty God. There is an active spirit world all around us, full of angels, demons, the Holy Spirit, the omnipresent Father, and His omnipresent Son, Jesus. The only reasons for me not to see this reality are unbelief or lack of knowledge.

In his sermon in Acts 2:25, Peter refers to King David's statement: "I saw the Lord always in my presence; for He is at my right hand, so that I will not be shaken." The original psalm makes it clear that this was a decision of David's, not a constant supernatural visitation: "I have set (literally, I have placed) the Lord continually before me; because He is at my right hand, I will not be shaken" (Ps.16:8). Because David knew that the Lord was always with him, he determined in his spirit to *see* that truth with the eyes of his heart as he went through life, knowing that this would keep his faith strong.

In order to see, we must look. Daniel saw a vision in his mind and said, *"I was looking...I kept looking...I kept looking"* (Dan. 7:2, 9, 13). As I pray, I look for Jesus, and I watch as He speaks to me, doing and saying the things that are on His heart. Many Christians will find that if they will only look, they will see. Jesus is Emmanuel, God with us (Matt. 1:23). It is as simple as that. You can see Christ present with you because Christ **is** present with you. In fact, the vision may come so easily that you will be tempted to reject it, thinking that it is just you. But if you persist in recording these visions, your doubt will soon be overcome by faith as you recognize that the content of them could only be birthed in Almighty God.

Jesus demonstrated the ability of living out of constant contact with God, declaring that He did nothing on His own initiative, but only what He saw the Father doing, and heard the Father saying (Jn. 5:19,20,30). What an incredible way to live!

Is it possible for us to live out of divine initiative as Jesus did? Yes! We must simply fix our eyes upon Jesus. The veil has been torn, giving access into the immediate presence of God, and He calls us to draw near (Lk. 23:45; Heb. 10:19-22). "I pray that the eyes of your heart will be enlightened...."

When I had quieted my heart enough that I was able to picture Jesus without the distractions of my own ideas and plans, I was able to "keep watch to see what He will speak to me." I wrote down my question: "Lord, what should I do about Rachel?"

Immediately the thought came to me, "She is insecure." Well, that certainly wasn't my thought! Her behavior looked like rebellion to me, not insecurity.

But like Habakkuk, I was coming to know the sound of God speaking to me (Hab. 2:2). Elijah described it as a still, small voice (I Kings 19:12). I had previously listened for an inner audible voice, and God does speak that way at times. However, I have found that usually, God's voice comes as spontaneous thoughts, visions, feelings, or impressions.

For example, haven't you been driving down the road and had a thought come to you to pray for a certain person? Didn't you believe it was God telling you to pray? What did God's voice sound like? Was it an audible voice, or was it a spontaneous thought that lit upon your mind?

Experience indicates that we perceive spirit-level communication as spontaneous thoughts, impressions and visions, and Scripture confirms this in many ways. For example, one definition of *paga*, a Hebrew word for intercession, is "a chance encounter or an accidental intersecting." When God lays people on our hearts, He does it through *paga*, a chance-encounter thought "accidentally" intersecting our minds.

So **the third key to hearing God's voice is recognizing that God's voice in your heart often sounds like a flow of spontaneous thoughts.** Therefore, when I want to hear from God, I tune to chance-encounter or spontaneous thoughts.

Finally, God told Habakkuk to record the vision (Hab. 2:2). This was not an isolated command. The Scriptures record many examples of individuals' prayers and God's replies, such as the Psalms, many of the prophets, and Revelation. I have found that obeying this final principle amplified my confidence in my ability to hear God's voice so that I could finally make living out of His initiatives a way of life. The **fourth key, two-way journaling or the writing out of your prayers and God's answers, brings great freedom in hearing God's voice.**

I have found two-way journaling to be a fabulous catalyst for clearly discerning God's inner, spontaneous flow, because as I journal I am able to write in faith for long periods of time, simply believing it is God. I know that what I believe I have received from God must be tested. However, testing involves doubt and doubt blocks divine communication, so I do not want to test while I am trying to receive. (See James 1:5-8.) With journaling, I can receive in faith, knowing that when the flow has ended I can test and examine it carefully.

So I wrote down what I believed He had said: "She is insecure."

But the Lord wasn't done. I continued to write the spontaneous thoughts that came to me: "Love her unconditionally. She is flesh of your flesh and bone of your bone."

My mind immediately objected: She is not flesh of my flesh. She is not related to me at all – she is a foster child, just living in my home temporarily. It was definitely time to test this "word from the Lord"!

There are three possible sources of thoughts in our minds: ourselves, satan and the Holy Spirit. It was obvious that the words in my journal did not come from my own mind – I certainly didn't see her as insecure *or* flesh of my flesh. And I sincerely doubted that satan would encourage me to love anyone unconditionally!

Okay, it was starting to look like I might have actually received counsel from the Lord. It was consistent with the names and character of God as revealed in the Scripture, and totally contrary to the names and character of the enemy. So that meant that I was hearing from the Lord, and He wanted me to see the situation in a different light. Rachel was my daughter – part of my family not by blood but by the hand of God Himself. The chaos of her birth home had created deep insecurity about her worthiness to be loved by anyone, including me and including God. Only the unconditional love of the Lord expressed through an imperfect human would reach her heart.

But there was still one more test I needed to perform before I would have absolute confidence that this was truly God's word to me: I needed confirmation from someone else whose spiritual discernment I trusted. So I went to my wife and shared what I had received. I knew if I could get her validation, especially since she was the one most wronged in the situation, then I could say, at least to myself, "Thus sayeth the Lord."

Needless to say, Patti immediately and without question confirmed that the Lord had spoken to me. My entire planned lecture was forgotten. I returned to my office anxious to hear more. As the Lord planted a new, supernatural love for Rachel within me, He showed me what to say and how to say it to not only address the current issue of household responsibility, but the deeper issues of love and acceptance and worthiness.

Rachel and her brother remained as part of our family for another two years, giving us many opportunities to demonstrate and teach about the Father's love, planting spiritual seeds in thirsty soil. We weren't perfect and we didn't solve all of her issues, but because I had learned to listen to the Lord, we were able to avoid creating more brokenness and separation.

The four simple keys that the Lord showed me from Habakkuk have been used by people of all ages, from four to a hundred and four, from every continent, culture and denomination, to break through into intimate two-way conversations with their loving Father and dearest Friend. Omitting any one of the keys will prevent you from receiving all He wants to say to you. The order of the keys is not important, just that you *use them all*. Embracing all four, by faith, can change your life. Simply quiet yourself down, tune to spontaneity, look for vision, and journal. He is waiting to meet you there.

You will be amazed when you journal! Doubt may hinder you at first, but throw it off, reminding yourself that it is a biblical concept, and that God is present, speaking to His children. Relax. When we cease our labors and enter His rest, God is free to flow (Heb. 4:10).

Why not try it for yourself, right now? Sit back comfortably, take out your pen and paper, and smile. Turn your attention toward the Lord in praise and worship, seeking His face. Many people have found the music and visionary prayer called "A Stroll Along the Sea of Galilee" helpful in getting them started. (You can listen to it and download it free at www.CWGMinistries.org/Galilee.)

After you write your question to Him, become still, fixing your gaze on Jesus. You will suddenly have a very good thought. Don't doubt it; simply write it down. Later, as you read your journaling, you, too, will be blessed to discover that you are indeed dialoguing with God. If you wonder if it is really the Lord speaking to you, share it with your spouse or a friend. Their input will encourage your faith and strengthen your commitment to spend time getting to know the Lover of your soul more intimately than you ever dreamed possible.

Is It *Really* God?

Five ways to be sure what you're hearing is from Him:

1) Test the Origin (1 Jn. 4:1)

> Thoughts from our own minds are progressive, with one thought leading to the next, however tangentially. Thoughts from the spirit world are spontaneous. The Hebrew word for true prophecy is *naba,* which literally means to bubble up, whereas false prophecy is *ziyd,* meaning to boil up. True words from the Lord will bubble up from our innermost being; we don't need to cook them up ourselves.

2) Compare It to Biblical Principles

> God will never say something to you personally which is contrary to His universal revelation as expressed in the Scriptures. If the Bible clearly states that something is a sin, no amount of journaling can make it right.
> Much of what you journal about will not be specifically addressed in the Bible, however, so an understanding of biblical principles is also needed.

3) Compare It to the Names and Character of God as Revealed in the Bible

Anything God says to you will be in harmony with His essential nature. Journaling will help you get to *know* God personally, but knowing what the Bible says *about* Him will help you discern what words are from Him. Make sure the tenor of your journaling lines up with the character of God as described in the names of the Father, Son and Holy Spirit.

4) Test the Fruit (Matt. 7:15-20)

What effect does what you are hearing have on your soul and your spirit? Words from the Lord will quicken your faith and increase your love, peace and joy. They will stimulate a sense of humility within you as you become more aware of Who God is and who you are. On the other hand, any words you receive which cause you to fear or doubt, which bring you into confusion or anxiety, or which stroke your ego (especially if you hear something that is "just for you alone – no one else is worthy") must be immediately rebuked and rejected as lies of the enemy.

5) Share It with Your Spiritual Counselors (Prov. 11:14)

We are members of a Body! A cord of three strands is not easily broken and God's intention has always been for us to grow together. Nothing will increase your faith in your ability to hear from God like having it confirmed by two or three other people! Share it with your spouse, your parents, your friends, your elder, your group leader, even your grown children can be your sounding board. They don't need to be perfect or super-spiritual; they just need to love you, be committed to being available to you, have a solid biblical orientation, and most importantly, they must also willingly and easily receive counsel. Avoid the authoritarian who insists that because of their standing in the church or with God, they no longer need to listen to others. Find two or three people and let them confirm that you are hearing from God!

The book *4 Keys to Hearing God's Voice* is available at www.CWGMinistries.org

Thank you for taking thoughtful time to read through Dr. Virkler's material. I pray that it will have an impact and be a blessing to you in all areas of your life. I encourage you to practice by using the four keys to answer the reflection question below. Once you start writing, keep writing. Let it flow. Don't be discouraged if you only get a sentence. It will get easier the more you do it.

1. Stillness: Be still and quiet
2. Vision: Focus your mind on picturing yourself with Jesus.
3. Spontaneity - Tune to the thoughts that are spontaneously flowing into your mind.
4. Journaling - Write down what you hear. Then go back and evaluate it when you are all finished.

REFLECTION:

Father, how do you see me?

____

____

____

____

____

____

____

____

CHAPTER 5

The Loneliness

I will never leave you nor forsake you.
Joshua 1:5

I hate the word "barren". It sounds so hollow and empty. Yet the word "infertility" sounds so clinical that it doesn't capture that hollow, empty feeling on the inside.

The pain of infertility is so lonely. You look fine and healthy on the outside, but inside you are broken – physically, mentally, and spiritually. You feel as if no one seems to understand the depth of your pain: the longing in your soul to hold a baby in your arms, the longing to create a new life that is part you and part your husband, to have the experience of becoming truly one through procreation.

Sometimes you can't even define why the longing is so great. Maybe it's because you have been dreaming of motherhood all your life. Then, when you're finally ready to take that step, you feel as if the rug is pulled out from under you.

There are so many different emotions that erupt: fear, shock, self-pity, anger, frustration, despair, denial, grief, hurt, depression...to name a few. All of them are negative. I understand. I felt all of those. I had to deal with them one by one. It took time. It's like peeling layers off an onion. Each negative emotion must be acknowledged and then released one by one. Nursing them, harboring them, dwelling on them, will end up with us in the proverbial "Pit of Despair". You don't want to go there. If you're there already - you want out.

The first year we tried to get pregnant on our own, my husband happened to be in seminary. That is a place where almost everyone is between 22 and 32. Many are married, and the rest are looking for a spouse. Those who are married decide to start families. They just do. So, here we were in an environment that I thought would be exciting. We'll all be pregnant together! How fun!

However, if you're the only one not getting pregnant, and I do mean the only one, it's not so fun. Even if *you* aren't in seminary, you have plenty of friends who are getting pregnant because you are at that age (or were when you were trying.) It's inevitable to be surrounded by baby announcements, gender reveals, baby showers, etc. It's hard.

I think it's important to understand that it's hard for your friends, too. They want to share their joy with you, but they know it will hurt. My best friend didn't tell me she was pregnant for weeks because she didn't know how. That hurt on two different levels.

One evening, I was at a meeting of women, and a friend announced that she was expecting their 7th child. It felt like a kick to the gut. She must have noticed my less-than-enthusiastic response because after the meeting, she called me and asked to come over. I said "Sure." She let me know that she was so sorry for my pain and wished she could give me a pregnancy. She acknowledged that she didn't understand my pain, but she realized her announcement was hard for me. Her kindness meant a lot. I assured her that she had every right to be excited about an expected child, and I appreciated her thoughtfulness.

Our friends hurt for us. Our friends hurt that their joy is dampened because of our sadness. Let's remember that. They want to be there for us, but they don't know how. But just because they are not experiencing the same thing as we are does not mean they can't support and love us through it. I had to learn to let my friends into my pain and not shut them out. Shutting them out just made me lonelier.

Ask God to send a friend in the same situation and support each other. Don't worry if they get pregnant before you. They understand.

When we started the adoption process, we met another couple at an agency open-house. We exchanged phone numbers and began to get together to support each other. That was so helpful! I thank God for Lisa and Gabe.

You see, the enemy wanted me to feel alone and isolated. That's his goal.

When I began to look at it from God's perspective, I could see where I had "stinking thinking," negative thoughts that lead to negative emotions. An important lesson in all of this is that Satan is our adversary. He comes only to steal, kill, and destroy. He wants to steal our joy and kill our hope and destroy our relationship with Jesus. It's his mission. Yuck.

But when we recognize that, we can begin to discern that the enemy is whispering in our ears, "You are alone. He has forgotten you," "No one understands," "God doesn't love you..."

Lies. All lies.

Here is the truth. You are never alone. *God will never leave you nor forsake you* (Deuteronomy 31:6). You are not the only one experiencing this.

The following is an encounter with our loving God that I

recorded in my journal during the season we were doing artificial insemination. Hear his heart toward me and know that it is the same God and same heart toward you.

> I got my period again this week, which was really hard to accept. Yesterday, I was at the breaking point. I lay down for an hour but couldn't really sleep. Just lying there, dozing and praying, helped me relax and calm down. I could feel God's peace begin to invade me. When I went to bed later, I was praying and dozing again when I felt a hand inside of mine. I thought Grant had come to bed, but I opened my eyes and he hadn't. I suddenly felt as though Jesus, himself, was holding my hand and saying, "I'm with you. I'll stay with you. You're not alone." What an experience! I fell asleep soon after feeling safe and secure. What an awesome God! What a loving Son! Thank you, Jesus!

You are not alone. Jesus knows what you are going through and what you are feeling. He can handle your grief, your sadness, and your anger toward him and the world. Give it to Him.

PRAYER:

If you're ready, here is a prayer for you to pray

Jesus, I don't understand why I haven't gotten pregnant. I feel so hurt, sad, alone, and angry sometimes. I know now that I am not alone. You are here with me. Please come in and take these feelings of sadness, hurt, anger and (add your own feelings here)

Come in and heal the wounds in my heart, mind, and soul that are causing these negative emotions. Help me sense your presence and love for me. I let go of blaming you for not answering my prayers the way I want, in the timing I want. Please forgive me for judging you as unfair and unloving.

I reject the lies of the enemy that I am not worthy, I am unloved, I am alone, God is unfair, and (add your own feelings here)

I declare these are all lies, and I will no longer partner with them. The truth is that I am a beloved child of God, and I am never alone. I can't do anything to earn His love or to make Him love me more. He will never love me less for any reason. Not getting pregnant has nothing to do with who I am as a person or child of God.

In Jesus' name,

Amen.

REFLECTION:

Do you feel some of the negative emotions lifting after praying the prayer?

____

____

____

____

____

Do you believe that God loves you unconditionally?

____

____

____

____

____

Do you believe that you are never alone?

____

____

____

____

Are you able to recognize the lies of the enemy when they pop into your head?

____

____

____

____

____

These are the negative feelings I have been experiencing...

____

____

____

____

These are the lies that I have been believing...

____

____

____

____

God's truths for me are...

____

____

____

____

CHAPTER 6

Anger

In your anger do not sin;
Do not let the sun go down while you are still angry,
and do not give the devil a foothold.
Ephesians 4:26-27

I can remember being angry. I don't know if I even knew at whom or what about. I was just angry.

I wasn't ever angry with my friends for getting pregnant. But I will admit being angry with God over friends who exclaimed they got pregnant "by accident." What?! The hardest was the single, female seminary student who suddenly got married and announced she was several months pregnant. What?!

Then I started thinking about prostitutes who got pregnant and women who had abortions. What?! How about children born to meth addicts and alcoholics and terrible situations? What?!

I went to an abuse shelter to minister to the kids there, and I thought, why were these kids allowed to be born into abusive situations, and yet I'm not getting a baby that would grow up in a loving home?

These were tough questions that I had to wrestle with. BUT - this was not for me to decide. By feeling this way, what I was really saying was that my wisdom was greater than God's and I was more deserving than they. Like it's a contest or something. But it's not.

What I'm actually implying is that God should have chosen me over them, like there are only so many babies to go around, and they might run out before getting to me. Not so.

God showed me I was judging their worthiness and acting like a Pharisee. Ouch. Matthew 7:1-2 says, *"Do not judge, or you too will be judged. For in the same way you judge others, you will be judged, and with the measure you use, it will be measured to you."* I don't want to be a Pharisee. I had to learn to let God be God and understand that He gave us free will. I am not responsible for how other people choose to use their free will.

After the night at the abuse shelter, God reminded me of a friend of mine who grew up in a severely abusive situation, so much so that she developed Dissociative Identity Disorder. He showed me how much He had healed her, how she loved Jesus passionately, and had become a beautiful friend. God redeems all things.

In analyzing my anger, I came to understand that anger is a manifestation of a wound. It is a secondary emotion that is a cover for the "real" underlying emotion. I was angry because I was hurt and jealous. Why would God not answer my prayer? Why wouldn't He choose me? Why would He choose them instead?

When I finally took all of that hurt and anger to God, I found healing and peace. I learned that "Why?" was not the right question. Most likely, I will not get an answer to that question. It is not for me to know.

"What?" is the better question. "What are you doing in me right now?" "What good will you bring out of this hardship?" "What do you want me to learn about You and Your ways?" "Who would you like to be for me in this situation?"

PRAYER:

Father, please forgive me for judging others and thinking myself better and more deserving than they are. I repent. Jesus, I give you these negative emotions of hurt, jealousy, anger and (add your own feelings here.)

Please come in and take them from me. I give them to you. Please come in and heal the wounds in my heart, soul, and mind that are causing these negative emotions. Thank you, Lord. Please show me what you are doing in me through all of this. Amen.

REFECTION:

What is underneath the feelings of anger? What is fueling the anger?

____

____

____

____

God, what are you doing in me right now?

What good will you bring out of this hardship?

What do you want me to learn about You or Your Ways?

CHAPTER 7

Laying Down My "Rights"

For to me, to live is Christ and to die is gain.
Philippians 1:21

In facing my anger, I had to admit that I felt I had a "right" to be pregnant. This right came from so many places and was probably further fueled simply by my being an American. We love to demand our rights!

As a woman, I had as much right to get pregnant as any other woman. It is the natural way of the world. It is how it is "supposed" to work. If a person not wanting to get pregnant can conceive, then so should I.

As a Christian, I felt I had a right to a baby. After all, I had been a "good" kid. My husband and I waited for marriage to have sex. Doesn't that count for something? We had been missionaries, he was studying to be a pastor, we were planting a church, we had given up owning a house and "expensive things" to go where He called us. We had been obedient even to moving across the country away from our families. What more did He want?

Maybe that sounds ridiculous to the outsider listening in,

but I confess that was honestly how I felt. God owed me this. It's ugly to type that out. I know it's wrong now. I was even fighting it at that time, but I couldn't quite shake the feeling. But here's what I love about God...He can take it. He didn't blow up at me, kick me out, forsake me, or anything else during that season. He gently showed me that He loved me. He was not punishing me for a sin, nor was He withholding good things to toy with me. He appreciated all of the good choices I had made in my life.

The Father waited for me to see that He owes me nothing. He gave everything for me - His son's very life. Everything I have comes from God. I owe *Him* everything! He appreciated my obedience and sacrifice, but they did not earn me favors. God's love and gifts are not transactional. His love is unconditional. He reminded me of the story of the workers in the vineyard (Matthew 20:1-16). Those who worked only the last hour got the same wage as those who worked the whole day. God's sense of fairness isn't ours. I have no right to demand my rights. God loves me and that's enough.

It was an ugly sin to admit and confess, but it brought freedom. It broke the hold that anger had on me. This resentment toward God for not giving me what I felt I deserved, not treating me fairly, was fueling the anger. Resentment is corrosive. It's like poison that slowly eats away at your soul and leads to self-pity and isolation.

I had to stop judging and blaming God. God had done nothing wrong. But my perception was that He had. I needed to say, "I choose to let go of blaming you for my infertility. I choose to not hold this against you, Father." Find freedom. Stop the poison.

If you think about it, nothing in this world is a "right." Everything we have comes from the Father. Every day we live and breathe is a gift from the Lord. We have no "right" to get married, or own a house, or be successful or even be happy. When we choose to follow Jesus, we choose to give up our "rights". We lay down our lives and take up our cross and follow Him. Laying down the right to get pregnant may be difficult. But I had to lay it down to move forward. Laying it down did not mean giving up the desire. It did not mean deciding I wouldn't get pregnant. It did mean that I accepted the situation I was in as undesirable, but I stopped demanding that God or the world give me what I wanted. I gave up the victim mentality that I had been robbed. I cast off self-pity and the depression that inevitably accompanies it.

"Many are the plans in a [wo]man's heart, but it is the Lord's purpose that prevails" (Proverbs 19:21). Having a baby was our plan. What was God's plan? Maybe this infertility was not His plan. God never desires infertility, or cancer, or disease. Those things came with the fall of man in the Garden of Eden. But God's plan and promise is to work all things together for good (Romans 8:28). So the question may be, "What will God do in and through infertility? Jesus assured us that *"In this world you will have trouble."* Claim that promise because it's true, and we often forget it. But also remember the rest of the verse: *"But take heart, I have overcome the world"* (John 16:33). He can overcome infertility in so many ways. First and foremost, ask Him to heal your heart. Secondly, to heal your body.

Resentment could actually be blocking your healing. When we are demanding of God, we are preventing Him from doing what *He* wants to do in us. Surrender and yield to His ways and His timing and see what happens. No guarantees of pregnancy, but a definite guarantee that He will meet us where we are.

Prayer:

Father, I choose to stop blaming you for not answering my prayer for conception. I choose to not hold this against you any longer or demand my rights. I confess my sin of judging that you were wrong or unfair. I renounce that judgment. Please forgive me for holding on to this resentment toward you and demanding my rights to get pregnant in my timing, or at all. I let go of this resentment and ask you to come cleanse my heart, soul, and mind of any and all resentment and wrong thinking. I agree that I am free to let you be God.

Amen.

Reflection:

Jesus, this is what I feel is unfair...

____

____

____

____

____

Jesus, what would you say to me about these feelings?

CHAPTER 8

Obsessive Focus

Lord, you are the God who saves me;
day and night I cry out to you.
May my prayer come before you;
turn your ear to my cry.
Psalm 88:1-2

In rereading my journals from the first year of trying to get pregnant, I can see that I was obsessing on this issue. I even say that about myself in those pages. It was literally the most important thing in my life. My mind was occupied with thoughts like... When am I ovulating? When am I expecting my period? Why isn't this happening? What can I do to help my potential? Who else is pregnant?

I surrendered it to the Lord many times, but had a habit of picking it back up again. It was such a heavy burden to carry. I began to see people as "pregnant people" rather than as my friend. I found that obsessing wiped me out emotionally and made me less focused on loving the people around me.

The world began to revolve around me and my needs. I could not understand why I wasn't getting more sympathy from those around me. However, in hindsight, this was a blessing, or I would have sunk deeper into the pit of self-pity. And it is a pit. I was definitely there at times. When you're down in that pit, the world looks dark. The way out looks too high and steep, and the enemy tells you it's comfortable down there. He says it is much easier to stay there than to make the effort to climb your way out.

But here is the good news. You don't have to climb out of the pit on your own strength. There are several ways to exit the deep well of self-pity.

1. Surrender to God and ask for His light to shine in your heart and He will lift you out.
2. Accept what "is" and begin to focus on other people rather than yourself.
3. Rebuke the spirit of self-pity and tell it to get lost. Claim the truth that God is with you and has a plan. This is the express lane to the top of the pit.

I have personally used all three of these methods to find freedom and my way back out of the darkness and into the light. If you are feeling in a place of darkness, try the above methods.

I know that self-pity sounds so negative, and we don't want to admit that's where we are. But take it from someone who used to be the queen of self-pity, it's so much better to realize that it is simply a trap of the enemy that you have fallen into and you will no longer be hoodwinked! *There is NO condemnation in Christ Jesus*" (Romans 8:1). Fight for yourself. Fight for your freedom.

Despair is also a dark, ugly place. It is a cousin of self-pity. Obsessing over an issue, self-pity, feeling helpless to change a situation - those can all lead to despair. We don't want to think about what despair leads to. If you are feeling in despair, please reach out for help. Go back and reject the lies listed previously. Cry out to God.

Again, focus on others and their needs. It really does help. Find someone who is struggling with illness or loneliness. Ask God how you can minister to them. Ask for eyes to see the needs around you. Part of our healing process was planting a church. We began to focus on the needs in our new neighborhood and the needs of those God sent to the church. That wasn't all we did, but it did help with the obsessive focus and self-centered world.

Surrender your will and your timing to the Lord. It's hard, I know. Do it over and over if you need to. That's what I did. Ask God what is *His* view of the situation. I wish I had done that sooner. Don't let this issue define who you are.

The definition of "despair" is to be without hope. There it is - the root. You need hope. God is with you, sister. He has a wonderful plan and purpose for your life. He is good and His ways are good. There is a beautiful future ahead of you and God is in it.

> *I lift up my eyes to the mountains—*
> *where does my help come from?*
> *My help comes from the LORD,*
> *the Maker of heaven and earth.*
> Psalm 121:1-2

PRAYER:

Father, I'm in a dark place. I don't want to stay here. I need your help and hope. Please show me the way out. I surrender the need to have a baby and the timing of it to you. I trust you. Your will be done in and through me. Please show me who around me needs your loving touch. Show me who to focus on right now to get my eyes off of myself and my own troubles.

(Out loud) I rebuke the spirits of self-pity and despair. I will no longer partner with you. Leave me in the name of Jesus! I am free to enjoy the other parts of my life and have hope for the future.

In Jesus' name,
Amen.

REFLECTION:

Father, what is your view of my situation?

____

____

____

____

____

Jesus, is there anything that is keeping me from fully surrendering this to you?

____

____

____

____

Who else can I focus on right now?

____

____

____

____

What would you say to me, Jesus, about hope?

____

____

____

____

CHAPTER 9

Identity

*"For I know the plans I have for you," declares the Lord,
"plans to prosper you and not to harm you,
plans to give you hope and a future."*
Jeremiah 29:11

I nfertility does NOT define you. This is not the end of your life or even your dreams. God has a purpose and plan for you.

Infertility made me feel less of a woman for some reason. That was probably the enemy, too. He is so sneaky. For many years, I felt left out of the "I had a baby club." You know what I mean. Every woman loves to tell the story of how long she was in labor and all the details surrounding the birth of her baby. Or they all compare notes on swollen feet and nausea during pregnancy. Even though some of these things sounded horrible, there was still FOMO (Fear of Missing Out). I wanted to experience that feeling of the baby moving inside of me. I wanted to know what it felt like to suddenly realize that I was expecting a baby! I wanted to experience childbirth and breastfeeding. I wanted my maternal instincts fulfilled.

After I adopted our daughter, I joined a Las Madres ("Mommy and Me") club at the local park. First question I got when I showed up was, "What hospital did you give birth at?" Ugh. That was in the parking lot. I hadn't even made it to the grass yet. As I joined the other women, they asked the same question. Must be a thing. I think I had thought I might be there several months before I would explain that my child was adopted, but no. All the women began opening their shirts to breastfeed. I got out Kristen's bottle and began to feed her. Immediately, I was attacked by questions of why I wasn't breastfeeding. I explained that my daughter was adopted. But that wasn't good enough - they began telling me about the Leche League, etc. All things I had explored, but weren't feasible in our situation. Not only did I feel left out, but I felt attacked. It was a bad day.

But guess what - I wasn't any less of a "mother" than they were simply because my daughter had not come out of my birth canal. They eventually saw that.

I still wish I had been able to experience all of that, but I no longer think of myself as "less than" because I did not. I am no less feminine than any other woman. I may not have experienced childbirth, but there are things I have experienced that others have not. Our experiences are all different, and they never define us. They shape us and affect us, but they do not *define* who we are at the core.

Another identity problem I had to get beyond was that word "barren." I am not barren. You are not barren. Barrenness connotes death and lifelessness. I am full of life! I am full of Holy Spirit! I bring life to those around me all the time. So do you.

Webster's dictionary defines "barren" as "incapable of producing offspring." I am not incapable of anything, because ALL things are possible with God! (Matthew 19:26). Not only that, I have produced spiritual offspring! I have many "children" in the Kingdom of God. As we share the gospel with others and disciple them, we bring people into a new life. They are our spiritual offspring.

The word barrenness has a finality about it, but nothing is final in God's Kingdom. He always has the last word. For all I know, I'll get pregnant at the age of sixty. (Don't know if I would want that, but God has the final say.)

So what is my identity? I am a Beloved Daughter of the King. My reality is that I never got pregnant, but that is my *reality*, NOT my *identity*.

*For I know the plans I have for you," declares the Lord,
"plans to prosper you and not to harm you, plans to give
you hope and a future." Jeremiah 29:11*

Hang on to this promise from God. It was given to the Israelites as they were being dragged off into captivity. Even in the midst of hard circumstances, He gave them hope.

I never got the biological baby, but God has given me so much and used me to touch so many lives. I am not finished, and neither are you. Your life is just beginning. You, as a woman, are more than just a baby factory. Get God's view of who you are. Believe what He says about you.

Prayer:

God, show me how you see me. Whisper to me the plans and purposes you have for my life. Thank you that infertility does not define who I am. Thank you that I am NOT barren. I am full of life and purpose. I have a beautiful future ahead of me. I am a daughter of you, King Jesus.

In your name, Amen.

REFLECTION:

Father, sometimes I feel left out when

Sometimes I feel "less than" in this way....

Father, show me how I am fruitful.

Jesus, how do you see me?

CHAPTER 10

Trying to Make it Happen

LORD, I know that people's lives are not their own;
it is not for them to direct their steps.
Jeremiah 10:23

At some point in this struggle, I think most of us give up the notion that it will just happen. We start trying to figure out how to *make* it happen. This is not meant to be a commentary on why you should or shouldn't seek medical help. This is the story of my journey. Whatever is decided should always be guided by the Holy Spirit. I'm not sure that I was at first. I was more driven by desperation. I don't recommend that.

I started my quest by learning to tell when I was ovulating. I used test kits and took my temperature. After months of no success, we went to the Ob/Gyn. Tests were run...nothing helpful. Then he started me on fertility pills and later shots. Those did not make me feel good. And alas, again – no success. By now, trying to get pregnant was becoming all-consuming. You know the drill – take your temperature when you first wake up before getting out of bed. Remember to take the fertility pills at the right time. Rearrange your schedule and try to feel sexy in the special window. Sex is more like factory work now. Then there's the agonizing wait for two long weeks – waiting, praying, and hoping for a miracle. Then it comes – the blood. Not just a nuisance anymore, now it is a heartbreak. I would break down crying in the bathroom at work; then, try to dry my tears and hope my red eyes and blotchy cheeks would not be noticed.

When the pills and shots did not work, we upped trying to make it happen. Next step – artificial insemination. Boy – isn't that fun? Suddenly, on the day when I was ovulating, everything had to be rearranged in both my schedule and my husband's. He had to "produce sperm" (factory work again). Then I would lie down in a very sterile environment to be inseminated. As I lay there on the table, I kept thinking – this is not what I thought getting pregnant would be like. I imagined a romantic night with my husband. I imagined it would just happen without doctors.

Each month that insemination didn't work was humiliating. Since I had to spontaneously leave work for multiple hours two days in a row for this every month, most of my close co-workers knew what was going on. I felt so guilty for my husband having to go through this month after month. At the end of seven months of insemination, we moved to a new city, and we decided to stop trying. We had no money or insurance coverage for In Vitro Fertilization (IVF). Also, the ethical implications of IVF were a bit overwhelming, and we did not know how to navigate them. I am not saying it is not a good option, because I've since learned how many people handle it.

After all that trying – I felt emptier than I already did as a "barren" woman.

Do you relate?

Moving caused us to reevaluate everything. Why were we trying so hard? Were we heading toward creating an Ishmael? I finally came to the conclusion that I was motivated as much by fear of never having children as I was by a desire to have them.

Fear is often what drives controlling behavior. Fear and wanting to avoid shame, failure, disappointment, and heartache. Fear drives us to seize control of the situation and try to make things happen. Fear is not of God. Control is not submission to God.

Control says, "Gee, God, I guess you need a little help here. No problem, I can take care of it on my own." or "God, you are not doing it the way I'd like. Just step aside, please and let me do it my way."

Of course, we don't think that consciously, but that is really what we are believing when we try to make things happen. I was queen of this. I was used to making things happen. I was good at it. But despite reading books, using ovulation kits, trying different techniques, artificial insemination for seven months, prayer, and anything else anyone told me about, I could not make conception happen. Only God could.

I got some great advice from my new ob/gyn. He talked to me about IVF. I told him that we did not have insurance that covered that, but also, we were uncomfortable with the ethical ramifications of destroying extra embryos or aborting babies if too many survived. He proceeded to tell me a story of a couple with similar concerns. He said they took only two eggs from her, fertilized them, and implanted them so that at most she would have twins. Both embryos survived, split in two and she had quadruplets. Then he looked at me and said, "Let God be God."

That really stuck with me. Let God be God. Not Anne be God. So that is what we began to do. We let God be God.

Remember the story of Sarah? After a while of God's

promise not being fulfilled, she decided that God needed a little help with a descendant for Abraham. So she gave her servant, Hagar, to him to have a baby for her. It worked - sort of - in that Hagar did have a son, Ishmael. However, it was not the promised son. But God blessed Ishmael to be a great nation, which has become the Arab peoples. There was enmity between Hagar and Sarah over the baby. There was enmity between Ishmael and Isaac. Their descendants continue to have enmity to this day, some four thousand years later. Wow! What a colossal mistake with huge repercussions.

Let's let God be God and not try to help him out.

PRAYER:

Father, I want a baby so bad that it hurts my heart sometimes. Forgive me for trying to make it happen in my own strength. Forgive me for seizing control of my life from you. Please guide and direct our decisions regarding intervention. Show us your plan and your path forward. Heal my heart from the hurt of losing my dream of getting pregnant easily on a romantic night with my husband. Please heal that wound in my soul. I let go of control and trust you with our family. Thank you, Jesus, that you do have a plan for us, and it is a good plan.

REFLECTION:

What is motivating our quest for children? Is it healthy motivation?

____

____

____

____

God, where do I need to back off from trying to make it happen?

____

____

____

____

CHAPTER 11

Fear

I sought the Lord, and he answered me;
he delivered me from all my fears.
Psalm 34:4

F ear is powerful. Negatively powerful. Fear can be a motivator for control. Fear is never a good motivator. Trust me.

Somewhere along the months of trying artificial insemination with no results, fear began to creep in. The "what if" monster began its destructive campaign on my mind.

What if you never get pregnant? What if your dream isn't fulfilled? What if you're super old like Sarah in the Bible when you finally get pregnant? What if you never get to be a mom and rock your babies and read books to them and sing to them and all the things you've always dreamed of?

Those are good questions to face in this situation. I had to move past fear before I could honestly face them. But how?

When I was sixteen, my mother died of cancer. It was

awful. It was like my worst fear had happened. However, I somehow thought that my trial in life had been early, and now I wouldn't experience any others because I "had mine already." What a ridiculous notion! So, when I wasn't conceiving, that fear of loss and trauma came on me strongly. I did not think I could go through another trial like that again.

Satan loves fear. He feeds on it. So he fueled it and fanned the flames until it grew into a formidable foe. But praise God, Jesus is bigger than the devil.

The one who is in you is greater than the one who is in the world,
1 John 4:4.

As this fear grew, it threatened to consume me. I finally decided to get on my knees and ask God for his perspective. I asked Him, "God, what is your will? Will I get to be a mom someday?" I clearly heard him answer "yes" in my heart. That was it. He did not say that I would get pregnant, and I was well aware of that. But the true desire of my heart was to be a mom, and he said yes to that. I could hang on to that promise.

That assurance helped me conquer the fear. I knew I still may not get my heart's full desire, but I had hope for motherhood someday. I knew it may not be in my timing or my way, but I accepted that.

Fear is NOT from God. Ever. Think about all the times that angels showed up to humans. They usually began with "fear not..." Second Timothy 1:7 tells us, *"For the Spirit God gave us does not make us timid [fearful], but gives us power, love and self-discipline."* God's spirit gives us courage. Fear is the enemy, showing us a picture of our future without God. Lies. All lies.

Psalm 34:4 was a helpful verse for me whenever fear snuck up on me. *"I sought the Lord, and he answered me; he delivered me from all my fears."* Bring the fear to Him and let Him shine His light on it. That fear will shrivel up and disappear in the light of God's goodness.

Fear is believing that God is not good, or God is not faithful. Think about it. Fear is believing that God will not come through or will somehow forsake us. More lies.

Whether or not you ever get pregnant or adopt a child, God has a purpose and plan and will be with you. He will not waste this trial you are going through or have been through. If you allow Him, He will bring good from everything we experience. This does NOT mean that He caused the trial or is withholding a child. More on that later.

The best way to fight trying to control things is to let go of fear and surrender the outcome to God. Get to a place where you can say, "It's OK if I never have a baby. I trust God's plan."

Here is a prayer I wrote in my journal in June of 1999 (two and a half years into our struggle).

Father, please show me how to surrender "getting pregnant" to you once and for all. Help me to let go and stop trying to make things happen on my own. I pray for the miracle of a child, but more importantly, I pray for the miracle of surrender. Please heal my broken, hurting heart. I want to minister from a place of wholeness, to others who are "broken." May I offer hope to others from my experience. Show me the way, Lord. May I want what you want. I love you, Lord. Amen.

If you struggle with fear, consider memorizing a few scriptures to speak out loud whenever you feel fear.

Here are a few to choose from:

For the Spirit God gave us does not make us timid, but gives us power, love and self-discipline, 2 Timothy 1:7.

I sought the Lord, and he answered me; he delivered me from all my fears, Psalm 34:4.

There is no fear in love. But perfect love drives out fear, because fear has to do with punishment. The one who fears is not made perfect in love. 1 John 4:18

PRAYER:

Jesus, please help me to let go of any fear. Take away my fearful thoughts and anxiety and silence the lies of the enemy. I choose to believe the truth of Scripture instead. I ask for your peace that passes all understanding to guard my heart and mind in Christ Jesus. I know that your perfect love for me drives away fear. You hear me and will deliver me from all my fears. Thank you that in you, I have nothing to fear. Thank you that you have given me a spirit of love and power and a sound mind. I will choose to trust you, whatever the outcome. Please hold my hand in the dark places and remind me that you are always with me.

REFLECTION:

What am I afraid of (specifically)?

____

____

____

____

Lord, in what way(s) am I acting out of fear?

____

____

____

____

Can I surrender this to God?

Dumb Comments & Awkward Moments

...take up the shield of faith, with which you can extinguish all the flaming arrows of the evil one.
Ephesians 6:16

I'm sure I'm not the only one who has encountered awkward moments. I suppose they are inevitable. But they aren't fun. Although I'm hoping that reading mine will forge a kind of secret sisterhood with you and give you a few chuckles. (Laughter is healing, so feel free to laugh out loud!)

One such awkward moment occurred at a birthday party for my daughter's friend. The guest moms were all congratulating the hostess, and I realized I was the only one who didn't know something. AWKWARD! I finally figured out she was pregnant. This was a fairly close friend of mine and the mom of my daughter's best friend. It was totally awkward, and I felt left out. Somehow, that made the news doubly hard. Feeling "out of the know" is such an awful feeling. It's something like having a 'Kick Me' sign on my back. And, yes, I've had a 'Kick Me' sign on my back before.

Then there are the awkward comments by people who don't know your situation. Maybe you've heard these...

- "When are you two going to *finally* start a family?"
- "Are you *ever* going to get pregnant?"
- "You've been married for *how long* and you don't have any kids?"

Or the ones from those that do know but think you're an idiot...

- "Have you tried seeing a doctor?" (Uh - gee - hadn't thought of that... LOL)
- "Have you prayed about it?" (Yes, but God is not a vending machine.)
- "Well, it just takes time." (Yes, I know. But "How long?" is the real question here.)
- "Stop trying so hard and you'll get pregnant." (wins "Most Common Dumb Comment" Award.)

My favorite from my brother....

- "You do know how to have sex, right?" (DUH!!!)

Then there are the not thoroughly "thought-through": comments...

- "Oh, how terrible for you!"
- "I would die if that happened to me." (I hope not!)
- "What's wrong with you?" (Wish I knew, but even if I did, it's none of your business

There are the nosy 'it's-none-of-your-business' comments...

- "Is it your fault or your husband's?"
- "How is your husband's sperm count?"
- "Are you doing artificial insemination or IVF?"
- "Do you have endometriosis?"
- "What did the doctor say?"

There are very few people who have the right to ask you those sorts of questions, and they are the type of friends who will wait for you to share and not ask. When you are asked these types of questions, you don't have to answer them. At first, I thought I had to answer, and it was embarrassing. Then I realized, "Hey, I don't have to tell them anything!" Best plan is to have a polite boundary reply ready. While I wanted to say, "What, are you a doctor or something?" I found it more polite to say, "I prefer not to discuss the details if you don't mind." Have a ready response, but don't get offended. Their insensitivity or nosiness isn't worth your joy. And, of course, they mean no harm.

Baby announcements and baby shower invitations are a bit awkward, as well. You want to be super happy for them and you are, but it's like being happy that someone gave you a beautiful rose, but when you take it, a thorn pricks your finger and you bleed, just a little bit. It's a Both/And. That's a lot of what infertility is. Both/And. There is Both anticipation And disappointment. There is Both sexual fun And clinic visits. Both happiness for friends And heartache for yourself. There is Both self-pity And learning to get beyond yourself. No wonder it's awkward to navigate!

If we can remember that our "situation" is just as awkward for our friends as it is for us, then we can learn to sit back and laugh. At first, the volume of baby announcements and shower invitations did me in. Then, when I realized that it was actually happening once per week, I shared it with my husband, who didn't believe me. Then it became a game to see if it was true, and we would write it down. Yep - there was a baby born this week. Oh, this week, so and so announced they are pregnant. We began to guess what the baby announcement of the week might be. We had to laugh at the ridiculousness of the situation. Even my sister and Grant's sister had babies in back-to-back weeks! I am not joking.

I found that having a response ready for those awkward moments was helpful. If I could think through what I was going to say before I was asked, then I wouldn't be caught off-guard. Maybe it is something that can put the other person at ease. What would Jesus say?

Side note: adoption brought more awkward situations. One in particular was how many people asked me where my daughter got her red hair (since I don't have red hair). I got very tired of that question. I did not feel the need to explain to complete strangers that she was adopted. Anyway, one day a woman asked me if my daughter's red hair was from her father. I wanted so badly to say, "I don't know. I never met him!" It was so close to slipping out of my mouth. What a lovely reaction that would have brought! But at least I could amuse myself and have a good laugh.

Last story - this one was really bizarre and awful. Hopefully, I can laugh at it now. One of the female seminary students came to me and said, "I hear you have something to tell me." I had absolutely zero idea what she was talking about. It was one of those weird conversations when the other person insists that you do know what they are talking about, no matter how many times you protest. After doing that back and forth several times, I asked her if she could tell me what she thought

I was going to tell her. She said, "You're pregnant and you didn't tell me."

That felt like a sucker punch. I said that I was not pregnant. She questioned my truthfulness. I explained that I had been trying to get pregnant for over a year but had not been able to. She turned sympathetic at that point. Turns out she couldn't have children either because she had her uterus removed as a teen. Then I had to ask who was spreading this rumor, and she agreed to go set that person straight.

It was all a misunderstanding, but talk about awkward...

At some point, we have to realize that all these dumb comments and awkward moments are traps set for us by the enemy. He wants to drag us down into depression and bitterness.

Don't let him!

Ultimately, remember that your friends love you and hurt for you. The acquaintances that say stupid stuff? Who cares! That is probably why they are not your close friends. If there is anyone who consistently makes you feel bad, don't hang around them. You don't need that. If you need to take a break from a group that is hard for you, then take a break. But whatever you do, do not forsake your support group or God. You need them. Desperately.

PRAYER:

Father, I hate those awkward moments and unthinking comments. Be my shield of faith to protect me from the fiery darts of the evil one. Let the hurtful comments bounce off and help me discern the heart of the speaker. Give me the ability to laugh at awkward comments and feel your presence with me always. Thank you that you will never leave me nor forsake me. Carry me through this season. I know there is light on the other side.

REFLECTION:

What's a thoughtless comment someone has made? Can you laugh about it?

Are there some friends you need to not be around right now?

Are there friends you need to reach out to more and let them support you?

____

____

____

____

Lord, how should I handle those awkward moments and people?

____

____

____

____

CHAPTER 13

The First Roller Coaster

I say first roller coaster, because later I will refer to the "roller coaster of adoption" - a similar experience. But for now, let's talk about the roller coaster of faith and emotions associated with trying to get pregnant. Each month was anticipation and hope, followed by disappointment and heartache. It has a lot of ups and downs. Especially when getting medical help, our hopes rise higher then fall farther. Not to mention we might be on fertility drugs that really mess with our hormones and emotions. Then there are the usual PMS hormones. Our poor husbands! Not only are they dealing with infertility, but they have to live with us! Add to that self-pity and we're a mess!

As I reread my journal, I found that my faith kind of "roller coastered" as well. I had total faith in God and His abilities and His sovereignty.

Until I didn't.

I wanted my will. I wanted a baby! Now! I wanted my dream fulfilled. After all, Lord, you said *"Take delight in the Lord, and he will give you the desires of your heart"* (Psalm 37:4). Well - I've always delighted in you. And you said, *"If two of you on earth agree about anything they ask for, it will be done for them by my Father in heaven"* (Matthew 18:19). Well, my husband and I agree, and we're asking. (Back to laying down our perceived "rights.")

Then I would get my heart right and be OK again.

Until I wasn't.

God can handle our ups and downs. Thank God. He is not angry or frustrated with us, by our questions, our angst, or our anger. He is patient. *"The Lord is compassionate and gracious, slow to anger, abounding in love"* (Psalm 103:8).

Our faith is tested in these times. But the super great news is that we end up stronger! A verse that both challenged me and encouraged me during that season was James 1:2-4. *"Consider it pure joy, my brothers and sisters, whenever you face trials of many kinds, because you know that the testing of your faith produces perseverance. Let perseverance finish its work so that you may be mature and complete, not lacking anything."* This is a great verse to meditate on. It took me a while to understand how to count trials as joy. But it was a valuable lesson that served me well in future trials. I will absolutely say that this trial developed my perseverance, faith, and maturity.

I can remember what I said to my daughter in her young teen years when she was mad that God had not answered her prayer. She said, "How am I supposed to trust God when he doesn't answer my prayers?" I explained that He is not a vending machine nor Santa Claus. Then I said, "If I can trust

God, though he didn't answer my prayer for pregnancy or healing my mother, then you can trust him, too. My testimony of faith **despite unanswered prayers** is stronger than someone's faith because of their *answered* prayers." And I still believe that's true.

> *In all this you greatly rejoice, though now for a little*
> *while you may have had to suffer grief in all kinds of*
> *trials. These have come so that the proven*
> *genuineness of your faith—of greater worth than gold,*
> *which perishes even though refined by fire—may result*
> *in praise, glory and honor when Jesus Christ is*
> *revealed.* 1 Peter 1:6-7

Don't let this trial be a waste. Use it to grow in your faith and intimacy with God. There is nothing like trials to drive us to our knees and into the heart of the Father.

And have grace for yourself. If you're having a really bad day, take a sick day. Ask for a hug. Spend time with Jesus. Play some praise music or go for a walk, or curl up and let the tears come. Do what you need to do, then get up and try again. Understand that emotional trials can wear you out and leave you tired and unmotivated. Get help from a counselor or friend if you need it. There is no shame in asking for help. This trial won't last forever, I promise.

Count it all joy!

PRAYER:

Father, thank you for loving me even when I'm a mess. Thank you for being a light in my dark places. Thank you for using this trial for good. I know that "In all things God works for the good of those who love him, who have been called according to his purpose" (Romans 8:28). Be with me and my husband through all the ups and downs and help us come out shining on the other side. I pray that you would answer our prayers for conception, but we choose to trust you no matter what. I know that You love me. Thank you for strengthening my faith through all of this. I will trust you. Help me when I'm wavering.

REFLECTION:

Have I discussed with my husband my crazy emotions and questions of faith?

____

____

____

____

____

Do I truly believe that all things work together for good?

Am I able to trust God despite my circumstances?

God, how do I count this as joy?

CHAPTER 14

I'm Not Worthy

See what great love the Father has lavished on us,
that we should be called children of God!
And that is what we are!
1 John 3:1

Somewhere along the line, I began to question why God was not answering our prayers for a baby. Was it because I was not worthy to be a mom? Maybe God knew I would make a lousy mom and wanted to spare my children that. Maybe He could not trust me with a child in his omniscience. Writing this now, it sounds absurd, but I know I secretly had those questions at the time. Of course, I did not share them with anyone because they would surely tell me the "right Christian answer" - that they weren't true. But didn't circumstances say otherwise? Why else would He answer other people's prayers and not mine?

Am I worthy? I think it's a question most of us deal with at some point, whether or not it is related to having a baby. I remember feeling not worthy of my husband. Sometimes I felt like an imposter at work. I would think, "Someone is going to figure out that I do not know what I am doing, and it is all over." My suspicion that somehow, I must not be worthy, came from deep in my soul. It was not just from this situation. The crisis of infertility just resurrected or highlighted it.

This feeling of not being good enough, or that somehow I would let people down, has haunted me all my life. I get past it for a while, then it rears its ugly head. Where is this coming from? For me, it was from childhood and high school. I realized that on two separate occasions, both my mom and dad had looked at me with disgust and declared their disappointment in me. That fundamentally rocked me to my core and made me doubt who I was, deep down.

I had wonderful parents and grew up in a Christian home. All parents make mistakes, mine included. I hold none of this against them. In fact, I'm guessing I've made the same mistakes with my children. I am quite sure, looking back, that my parents were in no way disappointed in who I was fundamentally. That is just what my little-girl heart heard, and the enemy exploited. This is not about my parents; it is about me buying into a lie. My heavenly Father helped me to trace this back and find freedom. I asked God to heal those childhood wounds. In the appendix, I give you a quick outline of how to work through this, but you may want to seek help from someone else if that's not enough. Healing our hearts can be simpler than we think, and also sometimes quite complex.

If you feel that maybe, just maybe, you are not worthy somehow, please ask God to show you the root of that feeling and work through the healing exercises in the appendix. Whether or not you get pregnant, you need this freedom! It took me years to realize the heart of the problem. It took only hours to get free!

Unfortunately, besides the enemy whispering lies to us directly, sometimes he uses others. At some point, you may encounter someone asking you, "Do you have sin in your life that is blocking this?" Of course, I had sin in my life. Most people do. But it made me begin to question myself. "What horrible sin am I unknowingly committing that is blocking my prayer from being answered?"

Or maybe the enemy brings up some horrible sin of the past that has already been dealt with, but now he points to it as the root of the issue. His lies make for bad theology. Trust me. There is no harm in asking God, "Lord, is there anything blocking my healing?" If he shows something, then deal with it. If not, know that God loves us, warts and all.

It reminds me of the story of Jesus and the blind man in John 9:1-2.

> *As he went along, he saw a man blind from birth. His disciples asked him,*

> *"Rabbi, who sinned, this man or his parents, that he was born blind?"*

> *"Neither this man nor his parents sinned," said Jesus, "but this happened so that the works of God might be displayed in him.*

The religious people assumed that he was blind as punishment for his or his parents' sins. Jesus said, 'Neither.' It was so that God's glory could be displayed through him. In this life, malfunctions happen. It's a fallen world we live in. Sometimes the enemy attacks us, but God always has the last word. He is not a God who delights in punishing, sitting in heaven waiting for us to screw up, and then zapping us. If He were, we would all be zapped a lot more often. There are natural consequences to our sin and the sin of others. But Jesus paid the punishment that our sins deserve. It's like a "paid in full" receipt.

If you have a sneaking suspicion, like I did, that maybe you are being punished or that you are unworthy, please recognize this for what it is - a lie of Satan. The name Satan literally means "the accuser." Jesus said in John 8:44 that lying is Satan's native language: *He was a murderer from the beginning, not holding to the truth, for there is no truth in him. When he lies, he speaks his native language, for he is a liar and the father of lies.*

He will accuse you, attack your identity and security in Christ, and lie about God and you. Be discerning. Share your concerns with trusted friends or your husband and allow them to speak truth into your heart. Meditate on the truth in Scriptures. I've included a few below. The TRUTH will set you free!

Believe me when I say that you are worthy. Not because of anything you have done, but simply because you are God's child and Christ paid for your sins. God cannot help loving you. He cries with us when we are hurt. When I was discouraged, I would picture myself sitting next to Jesus, and he would put His arm around me and comfort me.

God taught me a greater truth through this. Not only did He teach me that I am a beloved child of His, no matter what, but he also taught me that I need not have a transactional relationship with him. I never have to perform for him to be "good enough" or "earn points" or favor. If I feel *"not good enough,"* then at some point I can feel the converse of that. I can begin to think I have *earned* my salvation or His favor. The door swings both ways, and neither is correct.

God loves us, period.

That's it. Bottom line. He loves us to serve others in His

Kingdom. He loves for us to praise and glorify Him, but none of that earns anything.

I did not realize that I had subtly begun to feel that I had somehow earned his favor with my works and sacrifices. As I was desperate to have a child, I began to recount all the wonderful things I had done for Him. Like that made Him obligated to me. (More on that in the chapter, "Laying down my rights.") God's love is unconditional. Period.

Always remember who you are and whose you are. Don't allow the devil to tell you otherwise. Here are some truths to meditate on:

Ephesians 2: 8-9 *For it is by grace you have been saved, through faith—and this is not from yourselves, it is the gift of God— not by works, so that no one can boast.*

1 John 3:1 *See what great love the Father has lavished on us, that we should be called children of God! And that is what we are!*

Psalm 139:14 *I praise you because I am fearfully and wonderfully made; your works are wonderful, I know that full well.*

Lord, what would you say to the women reading this book?

Peace, my daughter. Let my peace sink deep into your soul. Let it bring a sense of rest. Quit striving. Just be with me. Sit with me for a while and let me minister to your hurting heart and wounded soul. I see you. I see all your pain and suffering. I cry with you. There is nothing you have done to deserve this. There's no being "good enough" to avoid life's trials and hardships.

This is a life best lived with me, hand in hand through all the ups and downs, during the trials of life. I will never let go of you. I promise. And I promise that my ways are good. I have great things in store for you in your future. This is a time of preparation for what is ahead. Submit to it and lean into me during this season. I promise, we will make it through if you keep your eyes on me. Peter walked on water when he had eyes on me. He sank as he began to fear the waves. There is no fear in me. Eyes on me. Hand in mine. Heart open. We've got this.

PRAYER:

Dear Father, thank you that I am never alone. Thank you for allowing your Son to die on the cross for me so that I don't have to suffer the punishment my sins deserve. Thank you that you now see me through Jesus - righteous and holy. I know now that infertility is not a punishment but a trial. You promise to be with me through it and use it ultimately for good (Romans 8:28). Show me anything physical or spiritual that is blocking conception and give me the solution. Otherwise, I will rest in your arms and trust you. Forgive me for trying to earn your love or favor. I accept your unconditional love for me. I am worthy of your love simply because I am your daughter.

REFLECTION:

Do I feel like God is punishing me for something in my past?

____

____

____

____

Jesus, speak to me about my worth

____

____

____

____

Please go to the Healing Exercise in Appendix 2 at the back of the book and work through it for more healing of your heart.

CHAPTER 15

Jealousy and Self-Pity

A heart at peace gives life to the body, but envy rots the bones.
Proverbs 14:30

Jealousy is an ugly emotion. And its cousin - envy - not pretty either. I knew I "shouldn't" be jealous or envious of others, but I was at times. I think it's only natural in the flesh, so you've probably had those thoughts as well. No condemnation. Hopefully, this chapter will help you out if you, too, have fallen into this trap that often leads to self-pity.

When I began to realize that the root of the hurt I was feeling over a baby announcement was actually jealousy or envy, I could see it for what it was. It's important to call a spade a spade, as they say. When I treated it only as a hurt, it fed self-pity. Not helpful.

I began to understand that while it was OK to admit my loss and hurt, jealousy and envy are sins and were dragging me to the dark side. Recognizing and rejecting thoughts of jealousy (Why not me? Why them? It's not fair...) was very freeing. It's not me vs them. This is not a competition.

I don't get to decide who gets pregnant. Conception is not

a validation of a person's worth or value, so non-conception isn't either. Life isn't fair. As I began to think these thoughts of fairness, I became a judge. Which of course, is not my role. I have no right to judge another woman about whether she should or should not have gotten pregnant. But it is tempting... Don't be tempted to the dark side.

One way to avoid this temptation is to be alert and to bring your hurts immediately to God and ask him to take the negative feeling. Ask Him to come in and heal the wound in your heart and soul. He will.

If you don't, you may slip into the trap of self-pity. I ought to know. I spent about a year trapped in self-pity, and it was a dark place. Notice the word "pit" in "pity". Self-pity is truly a pit. The more you feed it, the deeper you dig the hole. You begin to not want to hear from anyone who doesn't feed your self-pity. The deeper the hole, the less the light shines in. Step out into the light before the hole gets any deeper. Set yourself free from comparing yourself with others and feeling sorry for yourself. Bask in God's magnificent love for *you*.

Another way to avoid the temptation of envy and judging is the renewing of our minds. James 2:12-13 says, *"Speak and act as those who are going to be judged by the law that gives freedom, because judgment without mercy will be shown to anyone who has not been merciful. Mercy triumphs over judgment."* That last phrase became a guiding star for me. I would repeat it anytime I was tempted to judge another. *"Mercy triumphs over judgment."* I'm so grateful that God's mercy triumphed over judgment in my own life.

When I reflect on God's mercy for me, it makes it easier to have mercy for others. I can show mercy for the single pregnant woman by buying her some diapers, by introducing her to a support network, or at the very least, acknowledging how hard it must be to be pregnant and single. Mercy is praying for the pregnant prostitute, for her soul, for her heart, for the decisions she needs to make, for the circumstances that led her into prostitution to begin with. This is so much better for my soul than judgment which leads to pride and/or self-pity. Simply put, mercy is showing compassion and grace. It's choosing to not judge, slander, or punish.

When we practice mercy, we get our eyes off ourselves and onto another. We begin to see them through the lens of Jesus' eyes. And when we do this, we will find we no longer want to judge them. Truly, "mercy triumphs over judgment."

The key is to truly find contentment in the situation you are in. You may not be able to change it, you may not like it, but to keep fighting it, or wishing for something else, will keep you in a cycle of discontent and disappointment. The apostle Paul tells us in Philippians 4:11b-12, *"I have learned the secret of being content in any and every situation, whether well fed or hungry, whether living in plenty or in want."* Strong words from someone who had been persecuted and unjustly thrown in jail. He penned those words while under house arrest! So, what is the secret of contentment he mentions? The next verse tells us - *"I can do all things through him who gives me strength."*

Each of you has a unique path that God has laid out for you. There may be surprises, ups and downs, twists and turns, and sometimes sinkholes, but God is with you through it all, using it all to strengthen your faith if you let Him. My advice - let Him.

PRAYER:

Father, please show me any feelings of jealousy, judgment, or self-pity that you want to set me free from. *"Create in me a pure heart, O God and renew a steadfast spirit within me"* (Psalm 51:10). Please forgive me for comparing myself to other women and judging them. Please forgive me for feeling jealous and envious of others' blessings. I accept the blessings you have for me and give you thanks for them. Thank you for not treating me as my sins deserve, but giving me grace and mercy. Keep me strong when tempted

REFLECTION:

Jesus, show me your view of my situation and future.

____

____

____

____

Who or what am I jealous or envious of?

____

____

____

____

Jesus, which of my thoughts are feeding self-pity?

CHAPTER 16

The Dark Night
of the Soul

I pray that you don't experience a dark night of the soul. With Jesus, I believe we don't have to. But I did. Thankfully, I didn't slip into all-out despair, but maybe you have. It's OK. Just don't stay there.

At some point, I felt despair that I would ever have my dreams of motherhood come true. This tested my faith in so many ways. God said, *"Be fruitful and increase in number"* (Genesis 1:28a), so, obviously this desire is aligned with His will. He said, *"Take delight in the Lord and He will give you the desires of your heart"* (Psalm 37:4). Where are the desires of my heart? I have delighted in you always, Lord. So many questions and so few answers. I can't see up ahead anymore. Where is the light?

I have learned that Jesus is always with me, and He is the light. When I can't see, it's a problem on my end. I thought I was looking to Jesus, but in reality, I was caught up in *my* will, *my* program, *my* desperate desire, *my* insecurities. I wanted what I wanted, and I didn't really want to hear God say otherwise, so it was better not to ask or listen. If I asked Him if it was His will for me to get pregnant and He said, "No," then all hope would be lost. I wasn't ready for that.

I already mentioned loneliness. I was lonely partly because I withdrew. I didn't want anyone's help because I felt they didn't understand. Self-reliance sounds strong and noble, but it's the opposite of what God wants for me in His Kingdom. He wants me to rely solely on Him - for everything. AND He wants me to reach out to others for support. These may sound like contradictory ideas, but they go hand in hand. Ultimately, God is our source for all things. However, He himself told Adam, *"It is not good for the man to be alone. I will make a helper suitable or him"* (Genesis 2:18). In Ecclesiastes 4:9-10, Solomon says, *"Two are better than one, because they have a good return for their labor. If either of them falls down, one can help the other up."*

People are God's hands and feet on earth. We are not to *rely* on people, but we can joyfully lean on and accept help from the people God sends to help us. When we isolate ourselves, we become an easy target for the enemy. Praise God that Moses had two friends to hold up his arms during the battle. We all need people to hold up our arms during times of trial. That means saying "yes" to offers of help and wisdom. That means trusting people and being vulnerable. That means being humble.If it seems really dark, ask God to show you the light. He will, if you look for it. I think there were two things that helped me come back into the light. First, as I mentioned earlier, I finally got the courage to ask God if it was His will for me to be a mother. I had faith in his answer of "yes."

Second, my husband and I rented a place on the beach for a

weekend and grieved the losses we were feeling. We cried together and prayed together. Then we did a hard thing. We intentionally gave our desire for a biological child, our plans, and our will over to God jointly. We surrendered. We chose to not hold this against God. Not that God had made a mistake, but we were mad at him and judging him, and so we let go of our perceived wrongs and laid down our judgments. We agreed to stop trying for a while and focus instead on what God wanted us to do. We asked Him to heal our hearts over the next year, and then we would pursue adoption if that was His will.

The freedom that we felt after that weekend was incredible. I don't think we felt it right away. I remember feeling empty and depleted, like I had been stripped and emptied. I just wanted to sleep. But slowly over the next few days, the healing took place and "life" returned. The dark shadow had been banished, and the light was streaming in. I could look at our situation objectively. My faith was catapulted to new levels as I began to trust in Him for His will in many areas, not just this one.

The bitterness and resentment had been drained and replaced by a feeling of peace. It's hard to have peace when I am harboring resentment and bitterness. I have to let go of the negative to make room for the positive. I have to declare my trust in God.

If you are currently in a dark place, take heart. There is light, and His name is Jesus. Surrender to Him. The crux of surrender is saying, "I want what YOU want, more than what I want." It is accepting what "IS" and letting go of "What-could-have-been." This brings healing and hope to your soul.

As part of our surrender, we made some other decisions for our family. This may not be right for you, but we decided to take an entire year off trying to get pregnant or looking into adoption. We were already twenty-nine and thirty, but it was the right thing to do. We didn't want any of our adoption decisions to be influenced by the grief of not having a biological child. We realized time is always needed for healing to take effect. Decisions made on a rebound are often poor decisions. Also, we had just moved to a new city and were called to plant a church, so we focused entirely on that. This was so helpful because getting our eyes off ourselves and onto the needs of others was the quickest path out of darkness.

When you are in a trial, it is an opportunity to learn a new aspect of God within your relationship. You can ask God, "Who do you want to be for me in this situation?" God showed himself as a God of compassion. I learned He was incredibly patient with me as I complained and fussed and whined. I found Him to be light in the darkness. May you find that, too.

You and your husband may want to take a weekend away together to process like we did. It's good to grieve and heal together. (There is a sample plan for the weekend in Appendix 2 for your reference.) It never feels like a good time to go tackle our hurts and losses, but setting aside uninterrupted time together in a new atmosphere is a great way to make space for healing.

And like us - maybe go do something that you can't do with children. We went on a mission trip to Morocco and then went to Tunisia to see a former exchange student who lived with us when I was in high school. What a memorable trip! Enjoy the freedom you have!

PRAYER:

Father, it is dark right now. I can't see beyond today. I am hurting and desperate. I don't know if I can lay down this desire for a baby. It's so much a part of me. But I don't want to live in the dark anymore. I claim Isaiah 61:3. You have promised me "a crown of beauty for ashes," so I ask now for you to take my ashes and make something beautiful as only you can. I declare that I will receive the "oil of joy instead of mourning" and you will give me a "garment of praise instead of a spirit of despair." To that end, I choose to praise and glorify your name. I choose to walk in the light as He is in the light and no longer fall for the enemy's trap of self-pity, which keeps me in bondage.

You are my freedom, Jesus. Hallelujah! Do a work of healing in my heart and my husband's heart. Show us your will. Your will be done, not ours. I choose to accept what is and let go of what I wanted things to be like. I surrender my womb to you. I surrender my future to you. I can trust you. Please send me friends to hold up my arms throughout this trial. I love you, Jesus!

Amen.

The Spirit of the Sovereign Lord is on me,
because the Lord has anointed me
to proclaim good news to the poor.
He has sent me to bind up the brokenhearted,
to proclaim freedom for the captives
and release from darkness for the prisoners,
to proclaim the year of the Lord's favor
and the day of vengeance of our God,
to comfort all who mourn,
and provide for those who grieve in Zion—
to bestow on them a crown of beauty
instead of ashes,
the oil of joy
instead of mourning,
and a garment of praise
instead of a spirit of despair.

They will be called oaks of righteousness,
a planting of the Lord
for the display of his splendor.
Isaiah 61:1-3

REFLECTION:

What is the hardest part of surrendering the dream of getting pregnant?

____

____

____

____

____

Lord, who do you want to be for me in this situation?

____

____

____

____

What beauty will you bring from these ashes?

____

____

____

____

____

Is there something we should go do that would be harder to do once we have children?

____

____

____

____

____

If you're not ready to surrender yet, keep reading; the next chapter may help.

CHAPTER 17

Crying Out to God

I cried out to God for help; I cried out to God to hear me.
Psalm 77:1

There will be days when your heart is near breaking. There will be days when it is near bursting with joy over God's loving-kindness. God can handle our anguish and questions. He can bring healing and perspective. In the book of Psalms, David and others give us a great example of how to pour out our hearts before the Lord.

In so many of the psalms, the writer starts out by crying out to God and telling him how he REALLY feels. But somewhere along the way, he switches to recounting God's goodness and character and ends with praise. This is a beautiful example of how to go from depressed to thankful. It's a pathway to beauty from ashes.

As I was working on this book, I came across Psalm 77 in The Passion Translation®, which I thought was beautifully worded and appropriate for those struggling with unanswered prayer. Written by Asaph, who served in King David's court, it's a great example of that pattern of crying out, but then choosing to praise God for who He is. Read it below with an open heart and identify with the psalmist. Allow the Holy Spirit to minister to you through it.

PSALM 77(TPT)2
A Cry to God

To the Pure and Shining One
Asaph's song of love's celebration

I poured out my complaint to you, God.
I lifted up my voice, shouting out for your help.

When I was in deep distress, in my day of trouble,
I reached out for you with hands stretched out to heaven.

Over and over I kept looking for you, God,
but your comforting grace was nowhere to be found.

As I thought of you I moaned, "God, where are you?"
I'm overwhelmed with despair as I wait for your help to arrive.

Pause in his presence

I can't get a wink of sleep until you come and comfort me.
Now I'm too burdened to even pray!

My mind wandered, thinking of days gone by—
the years long since passed.

Then I remembered the worship songs I used to sing in the night
seasons,
and my heart began to fill again with thoughts of you.

So my spirit went out once more in search of you.
Would you really walk off and leave me forever, my Lord God?
Won't you show me your kind favor, delighting in me again?

Has your well of sweet mercy dried up?
Will your promises never come true?

Have you somehow forgotten to show me love?
Are you so angry that you've closed
your heart of compassion toward me?

Pause in his presence

Lord, what wounds me most is that it's somehow my fault that
you've changed your heart toward me
and I no longer see the years of the Mighty One
or your right hand of power.

Yet I could never forget all your miracles, my God,
as I remember all your wonders of old.

I ponder all you've done, Lord,
musing on all your miracles.

It's here in your presence, in your sanctuary,
where I learn more of your ways,

for holiness is revealed in everything you do.
Lord, you're the one and only, the great and glorious God!

Your display of wonders, miracles, and power
makes the nations acknowledge you.

By your glory-bursts you've rescued us over and over.
Just ask the sons of Jacob or the sons of Joseph, and they will
tell you!
And all of us, your beloved ones, know that it's true!

Pause in his presence

When the many waters of the Red Sea took one look at you,
they were afraid and ran away to hide—trembling to its depths!

Storm clouds filled with water high in the skies;
cloudbursts and thunderclaps announced your approach.
Lightning-flashes lit up the landscape.

Rolling whirlwinds exploded with sonic booms of thunder,
rumbling as the skies shouted out your story
with light and sound and wind.

Everything on earth shook and trembled as you drew near.

Your steps formed a highway through the seas
with footprints on a pathway no one even knew was there.

You led your people forward by your loving hand,
blessed by the leadership of Moses and Aaron.

The psalmist goes from "deep distress" to "Lord, you're the one and only, the great and glorious God!" This is your pathway to joy and happiness. Reflect on the goodness of God in your life. Focus on what He HAS done, rather than on what He has NOT done. Begin to praise Him even when you don't feel like it. Recount His glorious works and nature. Thank Him for all He is and has done for you. Feel your heart grow lighter as you do. Below, I give you the opportunity to write your own psalm to God. I encourage you to do it as an exercise in healing. No one has to read it but you and the Father. May this prayer be a pathway to healing for you.

PRAYER AND REFLECTION:

My Psalm of Surrender Father, I am feeling so.... (Pour out your feelings to him)

____

____

____

____

Why? (Ask Him your deepest question)

____

____

____

____

Yet - I know that You are.... (Recount his character)

____

____

____

____

And you have done great things for me. (Recount his goodness)

____

____

____

____

Therefore, I will praise you. (Praise Him)

____

____

____

____

CHAPTER 18

God Comforts Us to Comfort Others

*Praise be to the God and Father of our Lord Jesus Christ, the
Father of compassion and the God of all comfort, who comforts
us in all our troubles, so that we can comfort those in any trouble
with the comfort we ourselves receive from God.*
2 Corinthians 1: 3-4

One thing I learned about God during both the infertility journey and the subsequent adoption journey, was that he was a God of compassion and comfort. When I reached out to him with an open heart, He was there for me. Sometimes I would just come and sit with him and cry. As a teen, I did this after my mother's death as well. There doesn't always have to be dialogue or working on our hearts, or repenting. Sometimes, He just sits and holds us in our pain, and it's beautiful. So many times, His presence comforted me.

Bring your pain to Him and sit with Him. Allow Him to pour out His lavish love on you and comfort you. My husband found these verses during our struggle, and they brought great comfort to us both.

2 Corinthians 1: 3-7
*Praise be to the God and Father of our Lord Jesus
Christ, the Father of compassion and the God of all
comfort, who comforts us in all our troubles, so that we
can comfort those in any trouble with the comfort we
ourselves receive from God. For just as we share
abundantly in the sufferings of Christ, so also our
comfort abounds through Christ. If we are distressed, it
is for your comfort and salvation; if we are comforted, it
is for your comfort, which produces in you patient
endurance of the same sufferings we suffer. And our
hope for you is firm, because we know that just as you
share in our sufferings, so also you share in our
comfort.*

God is the Father of compassion and comfort who comforts us in ALL our troubles. Isn't that a beautiful thought? And I love what comes next. He says it is so that we can comfort others with that same comfort we have received. When we go through hardship, we are much more compassionate with others facing trials. We are able to offer them the comfort and hope that we received through Christ. God also uses our trials to build endurance in us. Something we all need on this journey called life.

Reading the Psalms can also be helpful. David did a lot of crying out to God. Check out Psalms 23, 16, 34, and 46 to start.

One thing you will note is that even as David cries out to God, sometimes he begins with praise. Psalm 23: *"The Lord is my shepherd..."*

Psalm 16: *I say to the Lord, 'You are my Lord; apart from you I have no good thing...'*

Psalm 34: *I will extol the Lord at all times; his praise will always be on my lips...*
Psalm 46: *God is our refuge and strength, an ever-present help in trouble...*

Praising and worshiping God does multiple things for us. First, it puts our focus on God, rather than ourselves and our problems. Second, it reminds us of who He is and all that He can do. Third, it chases away the enemy that may be harassing us. I will often feel a lifting of my spirit as I worship and praise the Lord. Fourth, it draws us closer to Him and allows us to feel His presence and comfort.

You can put on worship music, sing, dance, or all of the above. Try it!

Here are more verses to meditate on regarding God's comfort.

Psalm 103: 8-12 *The Lord is compassionate and gracious, slow to anger, abounding in love. He will not always accuse, nor will he harbor his anger forever; he does not treat us as our sins deserve or repay us according to our iniquities. For as high as the heavens are above the earth, so great is his love for those who fear him; as far as the east is from the west, so far has he removed our transgressions from us.*

Lamentations 3: 19-23 *I remember my affliction and my wandering, the bitterness and the gall. I well remember them, and my soul is downcast within me. Yet this I call to mind and therefore I have hope: Because of the Lord's great love we are not consumed, for his compassions never fail. They are new every morning; great is your faithfulness.*

Matthew 11:28 *Come to me, all you who are weary and burdened, and I will give you rest.*

PRAYER:

Thank you, Father, for your love and comfort. Please wrap your arms around me and help me feel your presence. Comfort this ache in my heart. Show me who I can comfort with the comfort you have given me. Let this trial not go to waste. Use it for your purposes and glory.

REFLECTION:

Lord, what words of comfort do you have for me?

____

____

____

____

____

____

____

Whom would you have me to reach out to with comfort?

____

____

____

____

____

CHAPTER 19

Hanging on to Hope

*Now faith is confidence in what we hope for
and assurance about what we do not see.*
Hebrews 11:1

Despair is the absence of hope. Despair is a dark and scary place. Despair is a terribly barren landscape that you don't want to visit. Hang on to hope.

Hope is like a lifeline that keeps our heads above water in a crisis. Without hope, we sink into despair. My hope that I would one day have children kept me from sinking into despair. So, from that perspective, hope is good. You can see people who have lost hope and slip into depression and despair. It's heartbreaking. Keeping hope alive can be critical.

But hope can be misused or misunderstood. I think at times I thought that hoping hard enough, or maintaining hope would somehow make it happen. That's not how hope works. Hope does not give us control - it gives us hope. Nothing more.

Hope can simply be an optimism about the future. I hope my team wins. I hope it won't rain today on our picnic. I hope her cancer is cured.

For hope to be more than optimism, it needs to be anchored in the right person and coupled with faith.

My hope for a baby was a wish, a strong desire, but definitely not a certainty. My hope was framed in doubt. I hoped it would happen, but maybe it wouldn't. Sometimes, I placed my hopes in the new medical intervention.

In one of my journal entries, I wrote how Romans 12:12 was helping me with hope. *"Be joyful in hope, patient in affliction, faithful in prayer."* This is a great trio. We can be joyful in our hopeful thoughts while being patient within the trial and always faithful to lay it before God in prayer. Hope can be a fleeting, fickle feeling when not grounded in God.

Our hope needs to be anchored to Jesus Christ. Once I realized my hope of happiness and fulfillment was ultimately in Him and His will for me, I had a firmer foundation on which to stand.

I went to a women's conference that had a huge anchor as the backdrop, and Hebrews 6:19 was the theme verse. *"We have this hope as an anchor for the soul, firm and secure."* Hope as an anchor - now I was getting somewhere. But this hope isn't anchored in conceiving a child; it's anchored in the unchanging nature of God's purpose. I could trust that His purpose for me was secure and would be fulfilled. Whatever it was - it would be fulfilling! And yes, it has been!

Here is the context of that verse, Hebrews 6:17-20

Because God wanted to make the unchanging nature of his purpose very clear to the heirs of what was promised, he confirmed it with an oath. God did this so that, by two unchangeable things in which it is impossible for God to lie, we who have fled to take hold of the hope set before us may be greatly encouraged. We have this hope as an anchor for the soul, firm and secure.

Then shortly after that, Romans 15:13 became a theme verse for me. *"May the God of hope fill you with all joy and peace as you trust in him, so that you may overflow with hope by the power of the Holy Spirit."*

God is a God of HOPE. Not despair. Not condemnation and punishment. Not death. HOPE. And He will fill me with JOY and PEACE as I TRUST in Him. So the path to joy and peace is trust. Wow. That was what I was missing. Trust. God wasn't answering my prayers. How could I trust Him?

I had to work through trusting Him again. I had to look at all the times God had guided, directed, and provided for us. I couldn't allow my current circumstances alone to decide whether or not I would trust God. Besides, wasn't God with me in this situation? Wasn't He comforting me and guiding me and growing me? Yes. I could trust Him EVEN WHEN I didn't understand.

This is a milestone in anyone's relationship with God; learning to trust Him in the dark - when we don't understand what is happening or what He is doing. That kind of trust builds rock-solid faith that will serve us well all our lives. It has built in me a foundation on which to build over and over again. And when I doubt, which I sometimes do, I can come back to all He has done *in* me and *for* me in the past.

For me to trust God again, I had to lay aside the fear that I wouldn't get what I wanted, or that what God wanted wasn't what I wanted. Fear is not from God. Ever. My doubt of His goodness or love for me had to be released. The Father is good, all the time. He loves me, all the time. Doubt had to be cast into the sea.

Back to Romans 15:13, after trusting Him and being filled

with joy and peace, THEN, I could overflow with hope - not by my own power, but by the power of the Holy Spirit. It's not about hoping hard or long; it's about trusting God and allowing His Spirit within me to fill me with hope. That's a pure hope. That's a hope that fills us with joy and peace.

In short, my puny hope had to be traded in for a newfound faith in a big, loving God. The God of Hope.

Hebrews 11:1 says, *"Now faith is confidence in what we hope for and assurance about what we do not see."* I had to find out what God's plan was and follow it, trust it, and believe in it. I mentioned earlier that I finally got up enough courage to ask God if I would get to be a mom and to truly listen for his answer, whatever it may be. At that point, I was ready to hear "No" so that I could move on. To my delight, He said, "Yes." Again, He didn't say I would get pregnant, but that I would be a mom. At that time in my life, hearing from God was not something I felt super confident in, so I didn't ask the follow-up question of pregnancy. I was content with the answer I got.

That was shortly before we let go of our striving to make things happen and took the year off. As my husband and I reflected, we recalled the night in his dorm room when we were discussing whether or not to get married, and we both shared our childhood desire to adopt children. I don't know many kids who dream about adopting children when they grow up. The fact that God had put that in both our hearts at a young age told us that He must have that purpose for us. We began to see that in a new light.

So, God's plan was for us to be parents. We could have faith - confident hope - in that. It seemed His plan was for us to adopt, so when we were ready, we could have faith in that as well. God has a plan for each of us. His plan is not always in alignment with our plan. Therefore, we need to get in alignment with His plan. Always the best option!

PRAYER:

Father, you are good, all the time. You love me and have a good purpose for my life. Please show me your will in all of this. I cast doubt and unbelief into the sea of forgetfulness. I will trust in you so that I may be filled with joy and peace and overflow with hope by the power of your Holy Spirit. I will have faith in the dark, when I don't understand, because I know the plans you have for us are good. They are plans to prosper us and not to harm us, plans to give us hope and a future (Jeremiah 29:11).

REFLECTION:

Father, where am I doubting your goodness?

Lord, is it your desire for us to have children?

____

____

____

____

____

Jesus, where do I need to trust you more?

____

____

____

____

PART TWO

Adoption Journey

A father to the fatherless, a defender of widows
is God in his holy dwelling.
God sets the lonely in families.
Psalm 68:5-6

You may or may not be thinking about adoption, but I encourage you to read this section. It will allow you to know my story, hear my heart during that season, and encourage you, should you choose that path. If you're unsure about adoption, maybe it will answer some questions you have. I will not, however, exhaustively cover the subject of adoption.

I thought that adopting would be the end of my infertility journey, or I think it could have been, but it wasn't. Read on to see how I had to lay this down more than once.

Back to our story...

CHAPTER 20

First - What Adoption Isn't

He has made everything beautiful in its time.
Ecclesiastes 3:11

Adoption is a beautiful picture on earth of how God adopts us into His family as part of His Kingdom. There is so much to learn through adopting a child into your family. But first, I want to address what adoption isn't, because I feel it is so important to understand before looking into the option of adoption.

Adoption is NOT a cure for infertility. So many times I heard, "If you adopt, you'll probably get pregnant," or "If you start the adoption process, you'll get pregnant." I even had several women tell me that happened for them, and that's great, but adoption itself is not the cure for infertility nor the cause of pregnancy.

Adoption is NOT an escape from the pain of infertility. Adopting my children gave me so much joy and fulfilled that longing to be a mother. However, I still desired to know what it felt like to be pregnant, to give birth, to breastfeed, etc. Those were issues that needed to be dealt with separately. Alcoholics think that getting drunk will help them escape their troubles, but it does so only temporarily, at best. The heart needs healing - period. There is no substitute for heart healing. Adoption has its own issues to deal with.

Adoption is NOT temporary. When you adopt a child, it is forever and ever and ever. Foster care is a way to "try out" adoption, but all other avenues are forever. This is important to understand so that it is not undertaken lightly. Just like we don't choose the personalities of our biological children, we don't get to choose the personalities of our adopted children. They are who God made them to be, plus what is inherited biologically and spiritually from their families of origin.

Adoption is NOT just like giving birth to your own children. It is not a *substitute* for childbirth; it's an *alternative* way to build a family. What's the difference? Adoption is its own thing. There is a misconception that once the adoption is complete and they are yours, you forget all about how they got there and go forward as if you had given birth to them. Some even try to hide the fact that their child is adopted. Don't get me wrong, I cherish my children and love them the same as if I'd given birth to them. I rarely think about my children being adopted.

However, adopted children do come with their own special needs. They need special love and security, and they come with a sense of loss that they need help working through over the years. Some children need counseling to come to terms with why they were placed for adoption.

Most adoptions are "open" these days, meaning that you continue to have contact with the birth family if they desire it. Both of our adoptions are open. We told our children about their adoption in age-appropriate terms when they were young, and established relationships with the birth families. We had visits with the birth families regularly at first, and more sporadically later on. When I first had visits with my daughter's birth mother, I was insecure and afraid. What if my daughter loves her more? Why can't I be her only mom? I don't want to share! These were deep insecurities that I needed to deal with. I am her mom. I'm the one who cares for her 24/7. She loves me. She can love her birth mother, too, and it does not diminish her love for me. I think the realization that no one can have too many people who love them really helped me get past that. What a blessing that my daughter and son have so many people who cherish them!

Lastly, adoption is NOT for everyone. Not everyone will be comfortable with the process, with the cost involved, or with the special needs. There are many types of adoption, and people are called to the different types, but it is a calling. BOTH the adoptive mom and dad need to be able to love another person's child as if he or she were their own. BOTH need to be able and willing to answer their children's hard questions about why they were adopted, because they will ask. Children of other cultures need to have their biological culture affirmed and celebrated. I recommend asking God if adoption is His plan for you. We felt sure it was for us because we had both had it in our hearts since childhood. We still did research and asked ourselves hard questions to make sure, but in the end, we felt it was God's path for us. May He guide you in deciding if it's right for you.

PRAYER:

Father God, thank you for adopting us as sons and daughters in your Kingdom. I know there are many children in the world who need loving parents and homes. You know our desire to be parents. Please give us wisdom as to whether or not it is your will for us to pursue adoption, and if so, which avenue. We trust in You and Your will for us. Amen.

REFLECTION:

Would I consider adopting, and why?

____

____

____

____

Father, what would you say to me about adoption?

____

____

____

____

CHAPTER 21

Before Adopting

He heals the brokenhearted and binds up their wounds.
Psalm 147:3

I never recommend beginning the adoption process while you are still badly hurting with infertility. Adoption won't deal with that pain and will only delay and sidetrack healing. Grant and I understood that we didn't have the emotional energy to jump right into adoption while still exhausted emotionally from trying so hard to conceive.

As I mentioned earlier, we stopped the medical intervention when He graduated seminary, and we had to move - over 2 years after we had begun trying. After moving, we went away for a weekend specifically to deal with this issue away from other distractions. We talked about our feelings and shared our feelings of loss. We got real and raw with ourselves and God. We prayed for each other. We journaled. We wrung ourselves out. It was a painful and difficult weekend, but it began the road to healing. We wrestled through our questions of why God was allowing this and chose to continue to trust

Him. We wept together and prayed together - a lot! We talked about the next steps for us. But I believe the biggest, most helpful thing we did was give it all over to God. We gave up our "have-to's." Heartbreakingly, we told God, if it wasn't His will for us to conceive, we accepted that. I remember letting go as if I were burying a mythical child.

We had to grieve the loss of experiencing pregnancy, being with our child during the formative 9 months, and childbirth. We had to give those into the Father's hands. We had to grieve the loss of a biological child. Adopted children don't share our genes, and they may not turn out like us. That's OK, but we needed to grieve that loss. Grieving takes time and energy.

When Grant and I decided to stop intervention and consider adoption, we did several important things. First, we decided to take a year off trying to get pregnant or looking into adoption. We needed time to heal from all the striving, heartbreak, and loss. This was wise, as the adoption process is very taxing emotionally, which we didn't even realize at the time.

Second, Grant and I shared our innermost feelings with each other. Sometimes, couples don't talk about the pain with their spouse simply because it's hard to verbalize it. We often think it's wrong to get mad at God, but He can take it. He wants to set us free of everything we have bottled up inside. If we don't let it out, it festers, and bitterness develops. Sometimes couples get divorced after dealing with infertility. I believe that is partly because one or both have let bitterness creep in and harden their heart due to heartache. Marriages thrive when couples are vulnerable with each other. Open up your hearts to each other and heal together. I truly felt free by the end of the year. (Later, things happened to bring up the issue of trying to conceive again, but at that time, I was content.)

Third, we decided to focus on Church-planting that year and to do something that we wouldn't be able to do once we had a baby. We joined a mission trip to Morocco and added on a trip to Tunisia to see the high school exchange student that I hadn't seen in the fourteen years since she had lived with us. That gave us something fun to plan and look forward to. When we returned from the trip, it had been one year since that weekend retreat. We began to research adoption. We were ready at that point. So much healing had taken place in that year. Taking a year off is a hard decision, as you've already spent years trying to start a family. In addition, the adoption process often takes one to two years. I was thirty by the time we started the adoption process. Despite all of that, taking the year to heal was the best thing we ever did. We got onto the adoption roller coaster in a healthy status, seeing adoption as a gift and not a bandage to stop the bleeding pain of infertility.

You are ready to adopt when you have God's green light, have researched it, talked to other adoptive families, and found healing from your deep, raw pain. (You may still long for pregnancy, but it's not an open, bleeding wound anymore. This means you can talk about it without crying.) You have taken time to heal emotionally from the infertility struggle and are excited about adopting, not seeing it as a second-class choice.

If the thought of adoption scares you, face your fears. Write them out. What are they? I had many fears and misconceptions before adopting. Grant and I went to the library and read many books about different types of adoptions. These were so helpful to clear up our understanding and familiarize us with the various types of adoption. Just briefly, here's a list of some of the options for adoption, though it is probably not exhaustive.

INTERNATIONAL ADOPTION

When you adopt a child internationally, the child is usually eighteen months or older. This option is the most costly, due to government forms for two governments, translations, airfare to foreign countries, paying adoption agencies in both countries, and more. It is not a "racket," it just simply is more expensive. However, the schedule is generally more predictable. These are not "open" adoptions, so that may be more or less appealing to some.

DOMESTIC ADOPTION

There are multiple ways to adopt domestically - meaning within the United States. First, there is contracting with an agency working with birth mothers. The agency helps put the two of you together and acts as mediator and counselor to both sides. In general, the birth mother has a short window to change her mind once the baby is placed with you and then the agency is the legal overseer for six months or so until the adoption is finalized in the courts.

Couples can also use an adoption lawyer in lieu of an agency to work with a birthmother. In many states, this option gives the birth family 6 months to change their mind and ask to keep the child.

Third, families can go the foster/adopt route. In that case, children of all ages are available for foster care and/or adoption. This requires being approved by the Social Services Agency, attending training, and obtaining certifications. Sometimes a family can foster and/or adopt siblings and have an instant family. Many of these children have been through abuse and/or neglect, and they need help healing from their past, as well as a new future. It's a ministry to that child, and you have to understand their special needs and be willing to sacrifice to help them. So needed, though! With all of these paths, a "Home Study" has to be done, which involves being interviewed and your home inspected to make sure that you are a fit family for adoption.

Lastly, some people "fall into" adoption when a family member can no longer care for their child and you, as their biological family, agree to adopt the child into your family.

I won't go into any more adoption information here, but know that if God calls you to share your love and home with an adopted child, it will be the best thing you ever did. Go into it with no regrets.

PRAYER:

God, my heart goes out to all the children in the world who need good homes. Please speak to my heart and my spouse's, and let us know your will for us regarding this. Help us face our fears and show us the path forward.

REFLECTION:

What are my reservations or fears about adopting?

____

____

____

____

Which avenue might we want to pursue and why?

____

____

____

____

____

CHAPTER 22

The Roller Coaster
of Adoption

He has made everything beautiful in its time.
Ecclesiastes 3:11

As I mentioned earlier, Grant and I both, as children and teens, had a heart to adopt children in our future. How good God was to place that in our hearts. Now, that doesn't mean that if you haven't "always wanted to adopt" that you aren't meant to do it. There are plenty of surprising things God has led us to do over the years. I could not have fathomed living in California when I was young. California seemed like the ends of the earth. But one day, I found myself moving there and stayed there for twenty-four years. Don't rule anything out until you have information and have taken it before the Lord.

Even with our heart's desire to adopt, we took it before the Lord to get a green light. We researched to see which avenue of adoption to pursue and prayed about adopting a baby versus a toddler or older child. All along the way, we felt the Lord leading us. As I relate our particular story, you will see God's fingerprints all over it. That's just how He works!

We decided that domestic adoption of a baby under one year old through an agency was our desire. We couldn't quite decide whether or not to go the birth mother or foster/adopt route. I naturally contacted the only Christian adoption agency in our area, which was about an hour away. They sent me information on international adoption. Since that was not the route we had in mind, we ended up not using them. (Turns out they did domestic adoptions as well, but God had other plans for us.)

My husband found an agency about an hour and a half away that worked with both birth mothers and social services. We drove there once a week for 6 weeks to take foster care training. Even though we never ended up doing foster care, we learned so much about adoption through that training. God knew what we needed. It took six months to go through the interviews, classes, paperwork, and home study.

One difficult part of the paperwork was all the detailed questions regarding what we were willing to accept in the way of a child, such as a child whose mother drank, or smoked, or used drugs during pregnancy. Or our willingness to raise a mentally or physically handicapped child, a child of another race, etc. It takes a lot of soul-searching and asking God's wisdom to know how to answer those questions. We talked and prayed about it a lot and then made decisions based on what we thought would be best for the child.

Once the home study was done and we had been approved, we moved to the next phase, which was waiting. Waiting is hard. And to quote a five-year-old, "It takes a long time to wait.[3]" There is no knowing how long the wait will be. When I say wait, I mean that we heard nothing for months on end. We just went about our normal lives, feeling a bit helpless, but at the same time cautiously hopeful. With pregnancy, there are body changes, due dates, milestones, and doctor visits to track progress and fill the time. But with adoption, nothing is happening but waiting.

I spoke earlier of the roller coaster of infertility, but adoption has its own roller coaster. While waiting, the agency would call out of the blue to tell us about an expressed interest from a birth mother or a possible match with a child in the foster system. They would ask if we were interested. If we said yes, then they presented our information to the birth mother or social services along with that of all the other couples that had said yes.

Then we WAITED - again. Our hopes rose - could this be our child? Excitement would build. Then we would get the call that they chose someone else. Crash. Down came our emotions. Heartbreak again. We would fight off discouragement and then start all over again. Grant and I always referred to it as the "Roller Coaster of Adoption" for this very reason.

In our particular case, we turned down a possible candidate from the foster care system as it didn't feel right for us. Another time, the agency decided an alternate family was more suited. Once, they approached us about a birth mother who was addicted to crack. We prayed about it and felt God leading us to say yes, but at the same time, felt that ultimately, she would choose another family.

We flew to Southern California to meet the birth mother and prayed with her. She chose the other family because she knew they had experience handling the special needs of a child born addicted. However, the agency told us how much it meant to her that she was able to choose, rather than going with the only family that would accept her child. It really ministered to her soul. God worked through us to bless her. It was still hard to hear a "no," but we knew that a baby exposed to cocaine in utero would likely have been very difficult.

We continued to wait. A year had gone by since being

approved to adopt, and it was January again. My birthday is in January, and I was depressed because I was turning thirty-two and still was not a mom. Our counselor called to check on me. I told her I was discouraged and asked if we should just give up. She encouraged me not to give up. I encourage you, too, not to give up. God does things in His own time, which is most often not MY time.

Like anything else wonderful that we are waiting for in life, adoption seems to take f-o-r-e-v-e-r. The waiting is hard. The roller coaster of emotions is hard. But once they are a part of your family, it is the most natural, wonderful thing in the world and worth all the waiting. Children are truly a blessing from the Lord.

PRAYER:

Father, I am grateful that all the children in the world are in your hands. You have a purpose and plan for each one of their precious lives. Please show us if we are part of that purpose and plan for a particular child. We trust you.

REFLECTION:

Do I trust God to be sovereign in the adoption process and bring just the right child for us and us for them?

Lord, what fears do I need to let go of in order to adopt?

CHAPTER 23

The Wait is Over

Your eyes saw my unformed body; all the days ordained for me
were written in your book before one of them came to be.
Psalm 139:16

When that one-year mark of waiting rolled around, I decided not to live my life on hold anymore. I made plans to visit a friend in China. My husband shared with me that a friend of ours had heard the word "February" while praying for us, and that might be God's plan. I wasn't convinced, so I bought the plane ticket. Thankfully, I have since learned to hear God and seek His wisdom.

However, on February first the phone rang, and it was my co-worker. She was so excited she could hardly speak. She had gotten an email that morning from a friend who had moved a few hours away. The friend's teen daughter had given birth to her baby five-and-a-half weeks early and they were scrambling because they still hadn't found a Christian family to adopt the baby. My co-worker just knew we were that family!

It was February first! Maybe this was a God thing. The

young woman looked at the website we had made and was amazed to find that we answered all of her wish list for a family. Only God could do that.

The next day, she called me. I immediately asked her how she was feeling after an emergency C-section. I also told her that I had been thinking about her and how hard this must be at the age of sixteen. She was being propelled into adulthood just like I had been at that age when my mother died. I understood the feeling a little bit. Later, she shared with me how much it meant that I cared about her and not just the baby.

I asked her if she was part of an agency and she said that she had been with the aforementioned Christian agency, but it had not been a good experience, so she had severed the ties with them. Now I understood that God had steered us away from that agency for her sake.

We made arrangements to visit later that week for an in-person interview with her. During the visit, we were so impressed by her maturity. We got to go to the hospital and see her baby in the NICU. She was doing well. I held her for the first time and absolutely fell in love. That was Tuesday. Thursday, I was at work and having a hard time concentrating. I hadn't heard from this young lady since the visit. That evening, Valentine's Day, she called me and asked us to be her baby's parents. That was my last day of work in the office.

It's hard to describe what I felt at that moment. First, relief and euphoria. Then, disbelief that this was real. Then, the realization of how much God loved us. It was incredible to see how we were an answer to her prayer, she was an answer to our prayer, and we would be a blessing to the baby. That's God's way – everyone ends up blessed in some way even, amid heartache and sorrow.

After the emotions settled down, I realized that we had none of the things we would need to bring a baby home from the hospital! We jumped in the car and went and bought a car seat and stroller. Thankfully, my best friend took me shopping at Target the next day for all the essentials.

On Saturday, everything was a go, and we drove to the hospital, got training from the nurses on caring for our preemie daughter, and brought her home. We were over the moon! I still remember sitting in the back seat of the car on the way home, next to this beautiful, peaceful baby in total disbelief that I was her mom!

The following day, her birth mom visited us because she wanted to see the baby in her new home. We understood. She visited again a few weeks later, and then we had a once-a-month visitation schedule for the rest of that year. The visits were a bit awkward for both of us, but that is where I had to lay aside my own feelings and do what she needed. I figured it was good for my daughter as well.

My daughter's name is another God story. Grant and I had been talking about baby names for a few months. I had a long list of girl names that I liked, and he didn't really like any of them (sigh). Grant finally found a name he liked, "Kristen." I liked it too, and the meaning is "Follower of Christ," so that was awesome. It was the only name he ever liked. When we first heard about our daughter, she had been named Kirsten Renee. "Renee" literally means "reborn" in French. What great meanings. In the end, we changed Kirsten to Kristen - just a switch of two letters. But again, how awesome of God!

Our daughter has now graduated college, and her life has brought us so much joy over the years. I cannot imagine our lives or our family without her. Knowing that God knew, back in September, that she would be our daughter in February, especially since she was due in March, is so comforting. He knew even before that because He prevented us from going with the local Christian adoption agency. God absolutely knows the plans He has for each of us. God has a plan for you and your family. Seek it out and let Him do His thing.

PRAYER:

Lord, I believe that if you want us to adopt, you have just the right child for us, and you have created us to be just the right parents for him or her. I will trust in your hand to guide us should we choose to adopt a precious child.

REFLECTION:

God, do you have adoption as part of your plan for our lives?

____

____

____

____

____

CHAPTER 24

Another Blessing

My frame was not hidden from you when I was made in the secret place, when I was woven together in the depths of the earth.

Psalm 139:15

After adopting our daughter, we decided we wanted to adopt another child. When she was a little over a year old, we started the process again, knowing how long it could take. I told the Lord that I really wanted them to be between two and three years apart so they could play together. They are almost exactly two and a half years apart. He took me literally! God is so good.

About July of 2003, we finished renewing the paperwork with our adoption agency and got "on the list." We had a few phone calls about possibilities, but none of them made it past the first phone call stage. Here we were, on the Roller Coaster of Adoption again.

In the beginning of February 2004, seven months later, I had a dream one night. (God sometimes talks to me in dreams, as He did to so many in the Bible.) In this dream, I was standing in front of a small roller coaster like you might find at a traveling fair. It was going round and round and up and down. (Already you see the symbolism.) A woman came up behind me and reached around and put her hand on my abdomen. She said, "Your baby will be born in eleven weeks." I looked down at my stomach and thought, "I'm not very big for being due in eleven weeks." Then I immediately thought, "Oh, she means we will adopt our baby that will be born in eleven weeks." Then she came and stood in front of me, looked me in the eyes, and said, "Yes, 'Sonny' will be born in eleven weeks." Then she disappeared. I thought to myself, "Do I have to name him Sonny?" Then again, I had an "aha" moment. I realized she was saying we would adopt a son.

I woke up, wrote down the dream, shared it with Grant, and we marked the calendar. Eleven weeks was the weekend of April 24th/25th. As that date grew closer, I became more expectant. On the morning of April 23rd, the phone rang. It was our adoption counselor. Before I thought about it, I said, "I was expecting a call from you!" and told her about my dream.

She was calling with two potential opportunities: a birth mother expecting a boy as well as a little boy that had just been born. We said yes to both. The agency felt strongly that we were the right family for the expectant mom. They showed her the photo album that we had made, along with albums of a few other families. She told us later that when she looked at the picture of our family, she suddenly "saw" her son's face in the family photo. She knew that we were the right family.

That Monday, she asked to meet us in person, and we went to meet with her and her mother. A day or two later, which seemed like a week, she called and asked us to parent her son. Again, we were over the moon excited. Our two-year-old daughter was running around singing, "I'm going to have a baby buther!" This time, we were a bit more prepared. Not only that, the baby was not due until July sixth.

One of the things we had prayed for this time around was that we could be present at his birth, since we had missed that with our daughter. Again, God graciously answered our hearts' desire. I drove an hour and a half with my daughter to attend the birth mother's doctor appointments. I was able to see the ultrasound and hear his heartbeat. This was an added blessing and bonus.

Our son, whom we named Josiah Grant, ended up being born a week late. My husband and I were able to be present at his birth and cut his umbilical cord. What an amazing experience! Once he was cleaned up, we went to see him in his little bassinet, and he reached up and grabbed one of my fingers and one of Grant's. It was such a special moment.

After being home from the hospital with him for a few weeks, my friend asked how many weeks it was from the time of the phone call until his birth. We got out the calendar and counted. Eleven weeks! Whoa. The woman in the dream, who, I felt was an angel, said eleven weeks twice. I had forgotten that. There were two sets of eleven weeks. There were eleven weeks between the dream and the phone call from the agency, and then eleven more weeks until Josiah was born. Our son can be assured that God destined him to be in our family. God makes no mistakes. His will and purposes are perfect.

I will be real with you, the moment of taking our baby home from the hospital, away from his biological mother, was difficult. I'm not going to lie. We felt a mix of emotions, including joy, awe, sadness, and even a tinge of guilt. Adoption is a blend of joy *and* sadness, hope fulfilled *and* grief, gaining *and* loss. It just is. There is no way around it. While we were giving our child wonderful security and comfort, it was important for us to realize that the baby was experiencing all new sounds and nothing was familiar. He needed extra comfort and care until he acclimated.

God is in adoption. I am certain that his first choice is for us to raise our biological children in nuclear families with a mom and dad. That is how He set things up. But God brings beauty from ashes. He takes what can be a crisis and makes it into a blessing. My children are truly a blessing. I am forever grateful to their birth families for choosing life, for choosing us, and for graciously doing something incredibly hard - putting their baby's needs ahead of their own heart. May God bless them a thousand times over for blessing us.

PRAYER:

Father, I am grateful that you know the future. The times and seasons are in your hands. Our future is in your hands, and it is good. Thank you for the many blessings you have already given me and all those yet to come. You are a good Father!

REFLECTION:

Lord, please remind me how you have brought beauty from ashes in my life.

____

____

____

____

____

Is there anything that is hindering my trust in You?

CHAPTER 25

Adoption Insecurity

Then you will know the truth, and the truth will set you free.
John 8:32

S ome of these chapters are difficult to write, because I hate to admit some things. But they are real, and hopefully they will help someone else who is feeling the same way. This is one of those chapters.

I love my children with every fiber of my being. I would lay down my life for them. I can't imagine loving them more if they came from my womb. But I am aware that they didn't come from my womb. I know that they will always have a spiritual connection with their biological family. I am their mom, and they love me as their mom. But they have another mom, their biological mom. I have to acknowledge that and accept it.

We have open adoptions, as I mentioned, so my children had contact with their birth mothers while growing up, but not their birth fathers, who were never really in the picture. I was very open to having their birth moms visit. I was so grateful for their gift and wanted to give something back. I recognized that their choice had been a painful sacrifice and wanted to do what I could to help alleviate it. I knew my children would benefit from the relationship, so I wanted it for my children as well.

But - to be perfectly honest, for years I secretly worried that my children would end up rejecting me and wanting their birth mother instead. I worried that Kristen and Josiah would love their birth moms more than me. Sometimes, I just didn't want to share. I wanted to be their only mommy. I knew that was selfish, but it was the insecurity preying on me.

Thank God that He never leaves us in those places. He is constantly stretching us and bringing us into new perspectives. And yes, correcting, convicting, and comforting us. Most of all, He brings healing to our wounds and insecurities.

I learned that love is not finite. There is not a finite amount of love that has to be divided up between people. Love is infinite. The more we love, the more love we have to give away. There was plenty of love from my children for both me and their birth mothers. This was not a competition. I didn't need to quantify if it was 60 percent me and 40 percent them. In God's economy, it is 100 percent each.

God helped me to see that these feelings stemmed from insecurity. And insecurity has its roots in old wounds and lies of the enemy. Satan wanted me to feel "less than." He told me I wasn't good enough. He wanted me to compare myself to other moms around me. Every mistake I made, he accused me and shamed me. He told me I didn't deserve to parent these children. I beat myself up daily and strove to do better. I read every parenting book I could get my hands on and tried desperately to be perfect. Bad idea. We will never be "perfect."

The turning point came for me one beautiful morning. I was in my bed, having time with the Lord. I was once again battling insecurity in parenting. Very humbly, I said to the Father, "I am so sorry I am not a good mom. I am trying very hard. Please help me do better." Then He spoke very clearly to my heart.

"Anne, who told you that you weren't a good mom? It wasn't me. Because you *care* about parenting well..... that makes you a good mom. If you weren't a good mom, you wouldn't care. Bad moms have no concern for how they are doing."

That was a defining moment for me. I was a GOOD MOM! I cared. I tried. I wasn't perfect, but that's normal.

Then - to put the cherry on top - Father, in his wonderful sense of humor, added this thought... "Besides, if you were perfect, no one would like you." Now there's a thought! None of us want to be around "perfect" people. We feel intimidated and discouraged. My imperfections made me real, likable, and approachable! How freeing! I could embrace my imperfections!

This freed me from my insecurities and comparisons. My children could love both me and their birth mothers in different ways, equally. What a relief.

That notion of not wanting to share, well, God had to deal with the selfish roots of that. But once I was healed of the insecurity, that didn't really bother me too much. When it cropped up (as I am human), I would have to call it what it was, selfishness. Sometimes we must crucify our flesh over and over again. (Or just remind it that it is already dead.) Putting others' needs and desires ahead of our own is hard, but in the end – oh so rewarding. Any time I have gotten over my own self-centeredness and sacrificed for others, I have been rewarded many times over. God is good.

PRAYER:

Thank you, Lord, for your infinite storehouse of love available to all of us. Please show me anywhere I have insecurity or am believing the lies of the enemy. Forgive my selfish tendencies and expand my capacity to give and love others as you do. You are good.

REFLECTION:

Do I have any areas of insecurity You would like to heal, Father?

____

____

____

____

Jesus, what lie am I believing?

____

____

____

____

What is the truth?

____

____

____

____

____

Jesus answered, "I am the way, the truth and the life." John 14:6

CHAPTER 26

Riding the Roller Coaster Once Again

But godliness with contentment is great gain.
1 Timothy 6:6

One year after adopting our son, my OB/GYN (a new one) gave me surgery for endometriosis. Of course, I hoped that this would solve my painful menstruation AND infertility, and I could also have a biological child. I remember someone asking me, "Don't you wish they had diagnosed this several years ago, before you adopted?" I was appalled at the question. Emphatically, the answer was, "NO!" I couldn't imagine my life without Kristen and Josiah. They are my children. How could I even contemplate them not being my children? God chose them for our family, and they were right where they needed to be.

I was content with my two children and had come to terms with not getting pregnant, though I knew there was always a chance that God would do something miraculous. I hoped He would, but I didn't expect it. In hindsight, I wish I had stayed in that mindset. It was a good place.

But...

First, there was the endometriosis surgery. That raised my hopes again. But after several months post-surgery, I realized that it didn't seem to solve the infertility issue. That was OK. I didn't really do the surgery to fix infertility. I did the surgery to heal the excruciating, debilitating pain of my cycle. I had lived with it all my life, but I found that taking care of babies and toddlers while incapacitated was not working well. Thankfully, the surgery relieved me of the pain. Hallelujah! So, it was a success. But I *was* disappointed it didn't have the effect of solving infertility, but that wasn't really the purpose.

And then...

We went to hear a prophet speak in July 2006, when my son was two years old. He singled me out of the crowd and spoke words over me. Part of what he said was this:

"He's releasing a new joy within the midst of your life. There's been a grief, because of the family dynamic in the midst of your family. I see where there might have been a desire for more family, more children, more freedom, more impact.

Now, that did not clearly say that we would have a baby, but one could interpret it that way. And we tentatively thought it could mean that. Our hopes rose a bit again.

But as usual, another year went by with no conception.

And then...

The following summer, my son turned three, and we were busy with potty training. One afternoon, I was joyfully helping my son wash his hands in the bathroom sink after helping him use the toilet. While I was leaning over him, washing his hands, I suddenly felt a burning fire in my middle. Instantly, I was alarmed and slightly panicked. What is happening to me? Is my appendix bursting? Am I dying? Then, just as suddenly, I realized that I was not in any pain. I felt the fire, but it wasn't painful. "That's weird, I thought." All the while, I am trying not to show any alarm to my son. As he dried his hands on the towel, I heard God speak clearly to my heart. "I am healing you." What?! "I am healing you," he said again. Then the fire sensation went away.

You can imagine what I was thinking and feeling. Euphoria! After all these years, God has healed my womb! I will finally have a baby. I told my husband, and my friends and family, who were all super excited for us. I let all those guarded emotions out of the bag again. I let my hopes soar. I mentally planned bunk beds and inventoried which baby items I had kept and what I would need to replace, as we had gotten rid of much of it.

A few weeks later, I got my period. OK. No big deal. It will be next month. But it wasn't. Or the month after that, or after that, or after that. We kept talking about the coming baby. We had told our children about my miraculous healing to build their faith. We started calling the child-to-come "junior," and we talked about when God would send the baby. These seemed to be acts of faith. In hindsight, I wish we hadn't. But experiencing a supernatural healing really does fill one with faith.

Surely God wouldn't give me that experience to tease me. Would he? To make matters worse, now I had friends and family following up with me. Are you pregnant? I thought God healed you. What's going on? I DON'T KNOW!!! Down the roller coaster once again.

It was so hard to know whether or not to continue to have faith or to once again let it go. I chose faith, but I also chose to just keep living my life. I did save all of my son's clothing because my husband heard God say it would be a boy. However, after about five years, we got rid of it all. Clothing just doesn't keep well. Styles change, mildew happens, time to let go. We got rid of the crib and some other items we had been saving. We figured it was better for someone to use the still-good items rather than storing them. That was a hard decision and action to take. It was like mourning the loss all over again.

People kept encouraging us, "Don't give up hope. God has a plan." I did have one "friend" who sat me down and told me to shut up about having a baby. She told me to be content with what I had and stop making my children feel bad. It was a horrible experience. In no way did I ever want to make my children feel bad. While I don't agree at all with how she approached me, I did listen, and we stopped talking about "junior." I buried him along with my hoped-for child, Grace Margaret. Another loss. More grief.

I don't tell you these things for sympathy. My only hope is to help anyone who may be stuck in similar circumstances or thought patterns. These emotional roller coasters are exhausting! But God never leaves our side. He helps us get out of bed each day and shows us all we can be thankful for. And, really, I think that's the key - thankfulness. Whenever I feel bad about what I don't have, I focus on what I *do* have, and that changes my heart and mind.

Through it all, I had to remember that God is fundamentally good. He does not "tease" me or lie to me or forsake me in my trials. He doesn't turn his back on me when I whine, or sin, or get angry at him. Bringing my focus off of myself and back on the wonderful character of my loving God kept me in the right frame of mind and my relationship with Jesus intact.

I stopped expecting to get pregnant, but I never stopped hoping. After all, Sarah waited fourteen years for the fulfillment of her prophecy. Though I'm not sure if I want to give birth at the age of ninety-something! Just saying...

As I began to enter menopause in my early forties, I realized that my time for getting pregnant was at an end. I began to despair. I had always had faith that one day, God would do it. He would open my womb and I would bear a child. Now, I doubted. I despaired. I went away on a retreat with my sister, and she asked the Lord what He would say to me. Here is what she wrote. I think God wants to say it to you, too.

I see you. I know the depths of your despair. I am right here with you. I have not abandoned you. I know your anger and frustration. I hear your cries for mercy. I know your fears and your doubts. I have seen your faith even when you don't understand and even in the midst of your frustration. I hear you. I see you. I know the depths of your heart, and all your unspoken words, fears and anxieties.

You are not alone. I have not forsaken you. You are my dearly loved child. Climb up into my lap and let me comfort you and heal your broken heart. I know your pain. You are not alone. You are not alone. I am right here with you. Come to me. I love you. Release all your hurts and all your pain to me, for I am the God who is with you. I will never leave you nor forsake you. I am here, closer than you can imagine.

Let those words soak into your heart, mind, and soul. Read them and re-read them. Make it His message to your heart. He loves you so much.

Do I believe that God heals and gives miraculous babies? Absolutely! I believe that His nature is loving and kind. I don't know why some of us don't receive the miracles we are asking for. I won't pretend to have the answer to that question. But through it all, hang on to the truth that God is innately loving and good. He cannot change.

Though I have ridden the roller coaster up and down many times, though I have wrestled with God and my own emotions and doubts, I write to you today as a woman who loves Jesus passionately with all my heart. I am free of bitterness and resentment and disappointment. I am content.

> *...I have learned to be content whatever the circumstances. I know what it is to be in need, and I know what it is to have plenty. I have learned the secret of being content in any and every situation, whether well fed or hungry, whether living in plenty or in want. I can do all this through him who gives me strength.*
> Philippians 4:11b-13

MY PRAYER FOR YOU:

God is loving and kind. Give Him your pain, disappointment, frustration, and anger. May you know God's everlasting, abundant, unconditional, never-changing love for you despite your circumstances. May you feel His presence beside you as you travel this road. May you find contentment and live out of that place.

REFLECTION:

God, what do you want to say to my hurting heart?

____

____

____

____

____

CHAPTER 27

Dealing with "Prophetic Words"

Do not quench the Spirit.
Do not treat prophecies with contempt but test them all;
Hold on to what is good, reject every kind of evil.
I Thessalonians 5:19-22

Earlier, I discussed dealing with the foolish things that people say to you. Remember - we try to laugh at those! But what about "prophetic words?" You may not be around people who share what God is saying to them for you, but undoubtedly, someone will say, "I just have this feeling..." or "I strongly sense..." I had all of these.

Once, I got a massage on a special Mother's Day Weekend, and the woman was asking me about having children, etc. Then she shared that whenever she was working on my midsection, she had the strongest sense that a baby would be born. That was encouraging!

I had another woman that I had just met on a retreat say to me as we walked together, she heard the Lord say that He would give us a biological child. She knew nothing of my story. I had just met her. Encouraging!

As I shared my healing experience with our pastor, he said the Spirit within him was giving confirmation, and he believed we would conceive. Wow! Cool!

So, how did I process those experiences at the time? All of these helped to build and sustain my faith for many years. As the years went by, I would sometimes feel cynical about them. (Not what I recommend.) My children had a Bible song CD, and there was a song called "God Keeps His Promises" about Abraham and Sarah. Honestly, I didn't like that song. I knew it to be true, but it didn't seem to be true in my case. At one point, I accused God of toying with me. Why would a loving God tease me this way? Why would He promise me something and then not deliver? It felt like the dangled carrot in front of the horse.

I had to work through this with the Lord. I had to let go of holding this against Him. I had to confess that His character is not one of toying or betrayal. Sometimes it is hard to hold an "AND" in our hearts. Maybe the words were true AND, yet didn't manifest for some reason. I had to admit that maybe it is something I will never understand while on Earth. There are many of those things in our lives. Why wasn't my mother healed of cancer? Why wasn't my best friend healed after God told me it wasn't "unto death?" I don't know. I probably never will. But I get to choose whether or not to continue trusting God, despite unanswered questions and experiences that didn't turn out the way I thought they would.

Another friend of mine who never conceived said she couldn't count the number of times people told her she would get pregnant. She even had twins prophesied multiple times! She has no answers either.

A prophetic "word" is when a person shares a message they believe is from God. I would say the majority of people who offer this to you are well-meaning and believe their message is truly from God. And it might be. After all, God gave me a physical healing and told me He was healing me, and yet I did not conceive. That does not negate that God actually spoke to my heart and did something in my physical body.

In 1 Thessalonians 5:19-22, the Apostle Paul gives us advice about this; *"Do not quench the Spirit. Do not treat prophecies with contempt but test them all; hold on to what is good, reject every kind of evil."* In other words, don't stop listening to the Spirit, and don't roll your eyes when someone offers to share what they hear from the Lord. But DO test what was given against Scripture and what Holy Spirit is saying to you directly. Keep what is good and throw out what is bad. Great advice!

After all, prophetic words are open to mistakes, interpretation, and changing circumstances. Our faith plays a role there, too, but don't blame yourself. Though the speakers may be sincere, they are human and not infallible. That's OK. We make mistakes, too. The hard part is that this type of mistake really hurts and messes with our emotions.

Before putting too much stock in a promise from someone else, weigh who is sharing this with you. Is it someone that you trust? Are they close to the Father's heart? Are they experienced in prophecy? Are they too close to you and just want it for you so bad that they may "hear" what they want to hear? Ask others what they think.

My advice - hold on to a prediction from someone lightly until you take it before the Lord. Ask Him if it is true. If you get a no, let it go. If you get no answer at all, continue to hold it loosely. If the Lord says yes, then declare it as true and have faith in what God said is true. Continue to speak it out loud over yourself and your husband. Pray in agreement together. Bind the enemy from stealing your gift. War for it. But only after God has confirmed it. Have faith. I might suggest not sharing it as widely as I did. Keep it to yourselves and your closest prayer partners.

Even though my faith did not "produce" a child, I learned a lot along the way. I could not control the outcome by believing harder. God is to be trusted, even when I don't understand. **I came to the conclusion that I would much rather have strong faith and not see the answer to a prayer than become a faithless cynic and be "right."**

Don't let unanswered prayers or prophetic words destroy your faith. God is trustworthy and good - all the time. I think the bottom line, again, is this: Do I want what *God* wants more than what *I* want? For a long time I wanted *my will* to be done. This second roller coaster of hope for conceiving was easier because I wanted *His* will over mine. I was filled with faith in God. Oh, there were many moments of crying out and moments of anger - I'm human. There were moments when Satan used it to mess with me. There were multiple times of grieving - again. But overall, I had the joy of my children and the optimism of more children on the way.

One difficulty was dealing with the embarrassment of having told people my story of the healing and then not getting pregnant. It was humbling. But I knew there were a lot of people watching how I would handle it, which encouraged me to go to God and handle it well.

Only God can heal these wounds in our hearts. When these trials come, the enemy encourages us to pull away from our Father. But indeed, these are the times to lean in and hear His heart beating for us as we lay our heads on His chest. It is the season to experience Him as Comforter and loving Father. Use the time to understand a new aspect of God's character and heart toward you. I grew a lot through all of these experiences. It's like the steel being hardened in the fire. Let these trials strengthen your faith, not destroy it; draw you closer, not push you away; build endurance and perseverance, not crush you. Jesus is by your side - always. He will never leave you nor forsake you. He cares about your heart.

I had a vision once of Jesus holding my heart very tenderly in His hands. He said to me, "You can trust me with your heart. I will protect it and be gentle with it." This is true for all of us. Visualize that in your imagination right now. Jesus is tenderly cupping your heart in his hands. He is good even when it doesn't feel like it. Remember that and hold onto it through the rough days. Don't let Satan whisper his lies to you. Recognize them and reject them. Put your focus back on Jesus holding your heart.

Consider it pure joy, my brothers and sisters, whenever you face trials of many kinds, because you know that the testing of your faith produces perseverance. Let perseverance finish its work so that you may be mature and complete, not lacking anything. James 1:2-4

PRAYER:

Lord, thank you for the loving people that you have put into my life to support and encourage me through this journey. Please give me wisdom when you are speaking through them and when you are not. Speak to my heart and let me know your will and how to pray. I trust you, no matter what.

REFLECTION:

Father, is there a "word" that I need to let go?

____

____

____

____

Father, what "word" do you have for me today?

____

____

____

____

What aspect of your character do you want me to learn through this time of waiting or unanswered prayer?

____

____

____

____

____

CHAPTER 28

Gratitude

Rejoice always, pray continually, give thanks in all circumstances; for this is God's will for you in Christ Jesus.
1 Thessalonians 5:16-18

Recently, a friend shared her experience of being sexually molested as a child. I looked her in the eye and told her of my deep sorrow that she had to experience that. She looked right back into my eyes and said, "Thank you for your heart and concern, but I am thankful for it. That experience has shaped who I am and has inspired me to help others through their pain." Wow! I was so surprised by her answer.

A few weeks after that, I was meeting a new person, and they shared that they had battled cancer for many years. Again, I expressed my sorrow at what they were going through. He looked at me and said, "Don't be sorry. It's the best thing that could have happened to me. It has made me appreciate every day of my life. It has kept me from drinking. It has made me aware of taking care of my overall health. It has drawn me closer to God." Again, wow.

Am I thankful for infertility? Yes. I cannot imagine my life without my two children, whom I adopted and whom I adore. They were meant to be in our family. God pruned a lot of entitlement, rights, self-pity, and other wounds from me in the process. God is good, all the time...even when we can't see it. God's word tells us to *"Rejoice always, pray continually, give thanks in all circumstances because this is God's will for you in Christ Jesus"* 1 Thessalonians 5:16-18. In James 1:2-4, we're told to *"Consider it pure joy, my brothers and sisters, whenever you face trials of many kinds, because you know that the testing of your faith produces perseverance. Let perseverance finish its work so that you may be mature and complete, not lacking anything."* God uses it all for His glory and our refinement. As Graham Cooke shares in his teaching, these are the times we get upgraded.

We may not like the trial, but we can rejoice over what it has produced in us – if that fruit is good fruit. God wants it to be good fruit. We simply need His perspective in the midst of it. Graham Cooke says not to ask "why?" but to ask, "God, what do you want to be for me in this situation?" He may answer, "Your sustainer, your friend, your healer, your provider," or something else. It helps to understand what He is wanting to reveal to us about Himself, and how He is wanting to grow us in our understanding of His character.[4]

At some point, I had to make peace with "the healing." I realized that God had said, "I am healing you," therefore He healed me of something. It may not have been infertility, but He healed me. Maybe there was something there I knew nothing about. So, I chose to thank Him for my healing, whatever it was. This was a huge switch from what I had been doing. I had been angrily asking him, "Why did you heal me if you weren't going to open my womb? It would have been better if you hadn't healed me!" Clearly, not the voice of gratitude.

More like the voice of attitude. So at this point, I made the choice to switch from attitude to gratitude.

Being thankful for a trial takes courage and a lot of healing. Are you at the point where you can honestly thank God for infertility? If not, ask for His help and perspective. It may require letting go of your anger toward Him first. That's OK. He can handle it.

If you're not quite there yet, that's OK, too. It took me years to get to that point. It's something to aspire to, and it's a marker. When you can authentically say you are thankful – then you are healed.

PRAYER (IF YOU'RE READY):

Father, thank you for all you have done in and through me during this trial of infertility. Thank you for showing me the ugly parts of my soul that need surrendering to you. Thank you for what you have done, and for what you will do. Thank you for refining my character and teaching me more about who you are. I am so very grateful to you for sustaining me through this dark and difficult time. Praise to You in advance for how you will use this to bless others.

REFLECTION:

What are the things I am thankful for in the midst of this trial?

____

____

____

____

What is keeping me from being thankful?

____

____

____

____

CHAPTER 29

The End of the Journey

Be still and know that I am God.
Psalm 46:10

I don't know if this journey has an end exactly, but I felt like my journey came to an end when I entered menopause. My period became erratic, and with it, I became frantic in some ways. What?! I had been waiting in faith, and now it will be too late! This means He isn't going to answer the prayer at all!! Oh, I know - remember Sarah... But as my period ceased altogether, I found it was time to let go and put this issue to rest for good.

Many years before, I mentally had a funeral and burial for my first hoped-for child, "Grace Margaret." While I figured that menopause meant no child, I didn't rule out that God can do anything. I didn't want to bury another child, "Junior." As I was talking to God about this one day, I heard him say, 'just leave him in my hands.'

So, I gave Junior into the hands of the Lord. He didn't seem dead. He was in God's hands. The idea of Him was safe with

God. I didn't have illusions that he was really in heaven with God. It was more like the promise, the idea, the desire, were all now in God's hand, not mine. I was letting go. It was gentler this way.

I was no longer imagining our family with this third child. I was no longer mourning the loss or angry about the delay or non-manifestation of the promise. I was at peace with it. God could do or not do whatever He knew was best.

I determined to place my unequivocal trust in God the Father, Jesus, His Son, and Holy Spirit. I accepted the fact that I would never truly understand what had happened or why things had not turned out a different way. "Why?" was no longer the question on my mind. It was unanswerable. I had tried to journal with God on that question in the past, but I had not felt that I was able to hear clearly from him on that. I guess, if I'm honest, on occasion the question will pop back up, but I've learned to tell it to go away. I no longer chose to wrestle with it. Now, I just quietly shut the door on it.

As I mentioned before, I realized that if I could testify to God's faithfulness when He hadn't answered our prayers, then my testimony would hold more weight than those who got what they asked for. Wouldn't it? It seemed so to me. When my daughter was struggling with an unanswered prayer, that is what I shared with her.

I had a very impactful moment when it felt like God was validating this for me. I was in the movie theater watching The Chosen, season 3, Episode 2[5], when there was a scene between Jesus and Little James. Jesus had asked the disciples to go out two by two and preach the good news of the kingdom and heal the sick.

Little James, who in this series has a disability, is concerned that he won't be able to heal others because he isn't healed.

Then he asks Jesus why He hasn't healed him. Jesus' answer is that the Father trusts him. They dialogue for some time on this issue, and it is beautifully written. Then Jesus puts his hand on James' shoulder, looks him in the eye, and says these words, "When you do great things in spite of this, the impact will last for generations."

It was as if I were alone in the theater with Jesus at that moment. The tears were streaming down my face, and it felt as if he were speaking directly to me. There was validation of the conclusion I had come to earlier, but there was also healing in my heart.

Watch that scene online if you're able. It's incredible and may touch your heart as much as it did mine.

Do I believe that God does heal and give miraculous babies? Absolutely! I believe that is His loving nature and kindness. I don't know why some of us don't receive it. But I do know that God is good, all the time! You can build your life and faith on that. If you are still in the waiting place - don't give up hope! God has a beautiful plan.

PRAYER:

God, there are so many things that I don't understand and maybe never will. You know how much I want answers. I lay down my desire for answers. I put this desired child into your arms for safekeeping. I choose to trust you despite how I'm feeling. I will proclaim Isaiah 55:9, where You say, *"As the heavens are higher than the earth, so are my ways higher than your ways and my thoughts than your thoughts."* I accept the fact that I cannot always understand your ways or thoughts. Thank you for all you have done for me.

REFLECTION:

Lord, what do you want to say to me about healing?

Who do you want to be for me in this situation?

CHAPTER 30

Conclusion

See, I am doing a new thing!
Now it springs up; do you not perceive it?
I am making a way in the wilderness
and streams in the wasteland.
Isaiah 43:19

It is possible to heal from this wound that feels so deep and raw. It takes time, and effort, and choosing the road to life. But – you can do it. God will walk with you hand in hand through this. Ask Him to walk you through to the other side.

God wastes nothing! There are my two children who might not be in my life if I had gotten pregnant. There is the testimony of feeling God's hand in mine. Something that changed my view of the Father's heart for a lifetime. There is the testimony to others of how God can take a bitter woman stuck in the pit of despair and self-pity and set her free, returning her joy, hope, and peace. There's the trading of control for trust, self-pity for contentment, and jealousy for genuine joy for others.

Pruning is never fun or easy, but the long-term benefits are worth every moment. So be sure to count the bright lights along the way of your dark journey. Record them as you go and let them be signposts to help you along the next leg of your journey. The sun always shines after the rain.

Ask God to send His wind to blow away the dead leaves of barrenness in your heart. I assure you, there are tender shoots of new life underneath. Water them, give them sunshine, nurture them, and they will grow into new, abundant life. Your heart matters.

Though you may feel empty now, you can still be fulfilled by the wonderful love of our heavenly Father. God loves you, and so do I.

"I have held many things in my hands, and I have lost them all; but whatever I have placed in God's hands, that I still possess"
~ Martin Luther

CHAPTER 31

For The Husband

WRITTEN BY GRANT TEAGARDEN

*Then Moses said, "Now show me your glory." And the LORD
said, "I will cause all my goodness to pass in front of you..."*
Exodus 33:18-19

The book you hold in your hands was hard for my wife, Anne, to write, even after all these years. It was hard for me to read and offer my suggestions, even after all these years. In all honesty, I did not want to revisit this. It stirred thoughts and feelings long left dormant, like going back to a desolate and deserted place you thought you'd never have to visit again.

This book was written to help your wife process the many thoughts and feelings associated with the journey of infertility; perhaps many that she's been afraid to acknowledge and share with others, maybe even afraid to share with you.

Anne has filled this book with her stories. Stories that your wife will likely connect with, and I pray that she does. I encourage you to pray the same because your wife needs validation that her emotions are real, that her grief is real, that people really do say some pretty stupid things, that God is present in the middle of all this, and that God is still good.

While stories definitely have a place, I'm simply going to give you, the husband, the bottom line up front.

- The grief is real... because the loss is real.
- It's not about getting over it. It's about going through it, together.
- It won't all make sense.
- Your Heavenly Father wants to help.

The Grief Is Real

The grief of infertility is seemingly odd because it is not the loss of something that was. It's the loss of something that was not. It is easy to try to discount the loss, to push it aside. But hear me, the loss is real. You must not try to simply push it aside.

Anne's chapter on "Grieving the Losses" presents it well from the woman's experience. The woman's loss experience encompasses so much more than does ours as men. God has a way of preparing a woman's heart for being a mom from a young age, including all the experiences leading up to the birth of the child. With infertility, so many of those experiences will not come to pass for her, at least not in the way imagined for so long. And that realization is a loss. It will be helpful for you to read that chapter. You need to understand the losses she is facing, losses you've never imagined before. It will likely be so much more than you would have guessed. You may feel some of the same losses that are mentioned in that chapter, but many of those are for women only. After all, I doubt you ever dreamed about what the closeness of breastfeeding would be like. But we as men still have losses. And some, your wife might never have imagined. And some may not hit you for years to come. As the years have gone by, here are just a couple of the losses I've sensed for myself.

- The loss of 'mini-me' kids. I'm not just speaking physically here (our kids actually do look a lot like us), I'm also referring to temperament, strengths, interests, and more. Though biological children are never exact replicas of the parents and often leave the parents wondering about some of their traits, there are always little bits of each parent showing up here and there. I had to let go of what I imagined that would look like for us. The two children God brought into our family are amazing. They are both creatives and are exactly who God created them to be. God bringing them into our family was part of His plan, and grace at work for Anne and me (see the chapters on our adoption stories, "The Wait is Over" and "Another Blessing"). Yet, through the years, I've had to release the thoughts of mini-mes to God. He constructed our family in a wonderful way. It was just different than I was originally expecting.

- The loss of a biological legacy. I'm the last of the biological Teagardens to carry on the family name in my little part of the family tree. My brother did not have children before his death. My sister has four daughters to carry on the family, but not the name. My dad was an only child and recently passed away. I'm now the 'patriarch' of the family, and my name-carrying little biological branch of the tree (I'm a ninth generation Teagarden from our ancestor in Germany) ends with me. That is no disrespect to my adopted children. Yes, my son can carry on the name, but he doesn't feel it the same way. And in the same way, I don't take offense from them in the fact that they are not interested in the Teagarden heritage. Teagarden family heirlooms, of which there are only a few, hold little interest for them, and understandably so. In my younger years, this was never of importance to me. Life was busy with the joys and challenges of shepherding a family, ministry, and an engineering career. But as a man ages, there is something about this aspect of legacy that surfaces in one's mind. It's something I have had to repeatedly give back to God. I am a dad to two wonderful young adults. I am a spiritual dad to others. Legacy can take many forms.

These losses are not purely unique to infertility challenges. Others can experience similar losses for a variety of reasons. The point is that these have felt like losses at times. To the degree you feel them as losses, to the degree your wife feels certain things as losses, they are real losses. Grief is the journey through.

Getting Through It Together

There are many wonderful resources to help people through the process of grief. My counsel is limited to your objective – for both you and your wife to get through it together. By together, I do not mean that you will process it in identical ways. What I do mean is that you realize this is a journey you both need to take, and it is best taken together. You really do need each other in this season. This is where your marriage vows, "for better or for worse, in sickness and in health," come into play. Grief is a sickness of the soul.

I'm a fan of *The Hobbit* book and movies. To me, grief can be likened to traversing through the dark forest of Mirkwood. If you aren't familiar with *The Hobbit*, Mirkwood is a vast, dark, and forbidding forest through which Bilbo (the main character) and the dwarves must travel to get to their destination. They are warned to stay on the path or risk getting lost forever. But the path through Mirkwood is winding and unclear. There is an ever-present sense of disorientation and fatigue. Signposts are lacking, and soon the travelers feel as if they are lost, circling back to where they have already been. Even time itself feels distorted.

Such is the journey through grief.

Anne and I mentor couples on marriage issues. We can tell you that a significant loss can really strain a marriage when the husband and wife struggle to walk through the dark forest of grief together. A typical pattern is for the husband to discount his grief, locking it away to reflect on as bite-sized pieces through the course of time. He may busy himself with new activities, finding solace in his ability to "fix" a few portions of his physical world, while processing bites of grief for those things he could not fix. He'll tend to process things quietly, internally, and usually alone. In view of Mirkwood, he may try to race ahead, to find a shortcut, to get out of the oppressive and disorienting dark forest as quickly as possible. He does not want his fellow travelers to make him stay in this forlorn place any longer than absolutely necessary.

His wife, in contrast, may feel the need to process all the emotions, to reflect on the losses wholeheartedly. She may feel compelled to stop and open up the box of emotions and losses, pulling out one after another, after another. Most likely, she does not want to do this alone. She wants her strong man beside her, holding her, reassuring her. She may prefer to process it externally – talking through each item in the box, mourning what will not be. In view of Mirkwood, she probably feels that rushing is precisely the wrong approach. The forest needs to be understood and appreciated for what it is, as dark as it may be. It must be experienced in order to follow the path out.

The temptation then is for the husband to view his wife as 'needlessly dwelling' in the pain, while the wife may view the husband as 'avoiding' the pain and 'not honoring' the losses. The strong temptation is for the two to separate in the forest, each leaving the other to fend for themselves. This is the temptation you must resist. Scripture reminds us that *"two are better than one... If either of them falls down, one can help the other up. But pity anyone who falls and has no one to help them up"* (Ecclesiastes 4:9-10).

As a husband, your objective is not to 'pull' your wife through her grief. Your job is to stay with her there – to not leave her alone. Your job is to support her journey, at her pace. If you want to speed the journey, make yourself more available to her. She needs your strength. You must want to support her there in Mirkwood more than you want to get yourself out.

Anne overviews our story of journeying through grief in the chapter, "Before Adopting." I recommend you read that chapter too. In short, we set aside a full year to process our grief of infertility. And we kicked it off with a weekend away, figuratively camping out in Mirkwood. On that weekend away, we opened our boxes of emotions. We talked. We cried. We prayed. We did our best to lay it all at God's feet, surrendering our hopes and dreams for biological children to Him. But most importantly, we did it together. That weekend away, along with the expectation of a year's journey through Mirkwood, set the stage for us to get through grief together. That is your objective.

IT WON'T ALL MAKE SENSE

I wish I could tell you that everything made sense once we emerged from Mirkwood, but that would be a lie. Grief is not limited in time. New losses are discovered. Questions remain. You don't emerge from Mirkwood all at once. The dreariness simply begins to thin out, with sunlight progressively filtering through, more glimpses of blue sky, and cleaner air to breathe.

The story of Job in the Bible has always fascinated me. Many Bible scholars believe it was the first book of the Bible to be written down, perhaps 50 to 500 years before Genesis was recorded. For many people long ago, this was their only written Scripture. One of my principal fascinations is the backstory presented in chapters 1 and 2. There, we get to read the cosmic court transcript behind Job's trials as Satan appears before God and His angels, asking permission to test Job's faithfulness and trust in God. God agrees to the test, withdrawing divine protection from Job and extending Satan's leash. Satan is allowed to destroy Job's ten children, all his wealth, and his health. It appears the whole spirit realm, through the court of heaven, was privy to everything that was transpiring. But not Job. Not his wife. Not his four friends.

The account ends in chapter 42 with Job repenting for pushing God for answers, Job's first three friends repenting for giving wrong answers, and God's double blessing upon Job's life. But still, even at the end of the story, it appears Job never knew why.

Anne and I still don't understand the 'why' of our journey, particularly after God gave an unanticipated healing touch to Anne's body (see the chapter, "Riding the Roller Coaster Once

Again," for that story). We felt a renewed hope, but *"hope deferred makes the heart sick"* (Proverbs 13:12). Once again, we had to let it go. We had to bring that 'heart sickness' to God for His healing. To put it all in His hands, trusting His goodness in our lives.

YOUR HEAVENLY FATHER WANTS TO HELP

In the midst of this entire journey, and in all honesty, even afterward, there is the temptation to doubt God's goodness. That, ultimately, is always from the enemy of our souls. Every temptation of the enemy is aimed at getting us to doubt God's good intentions for us. The reason is simple. We will never go for help to someone we do not trust.

The verses at the top of this chapter, Exodus 33:18-19, capture a startling, revelatory truth of Scripture. This event unfolds with Moses at the top of Mount Sinai. Prior to this point, God had revealed Himself to Moses in the burning bush. God effected his rescue of the Israelite slaves and established his power over the Egyptian gods by releasing ten plagues on the Egyptians while protecting the Israelites from the same. God visibly demonstrated His presence as He led the people with cloud and fire to guide their way. God strategically parted the waters of the Red Sea, dried a path for their escape, and then destroyed the pursuing Egyptian army in front of their eyes. En route to the new land, God provided manna and quail daily for the two million people to eat. Now, at Mount Sinai, thunder and lightning and smoke like a furnace cover the peak. Into this Moses goes to meet with God.

There, at the top of the mountain, Moses asks God to reveal His glory. It's a little hard to wrap our heads around what else Moses wanted to see from God. Most of us would love to witness firsthand just one of the miracles that Moses experienced. But Moses asks for more.

God's response is totally different than what anyone might have expected. God told Moses, "I will cause all my *goodness* to pass in front of you…" In essence, God told Moses, "The weight of My Glory is not expressed in this thunder and lightning and billowing smoke, nor is it through destroying your enemies. It's not about providing food from heaven. The weight of My Glory rests in My Goodness. From *this*, everything else flows."

When all else in life fails, the path forward starts with a renewed awareness and appreciation of God's goodness for you and your wife. You both have to feel it at the core of your being. The best way for that to happen is to hear it straight from Him.

In chapter 4, "Gentle Whispers," Anne presents material originally created by Mark Virkler on how to more clearly hear God's voice. This was a game-changer for our lives spiritually. Like Moses, we come to God looking for one thing, but God will start with what is most important – expressing His love and goodness for us.

When I first started to hear from God more clearly and more directly, the messages were short – "Grant, I love you." I said, "Yes, yes, I know that. Tell me something I don't know. I have lots of questions." The essence of his replies was simply, "Grant, that is the most important thing I can tell you. You don't know it well enough yet." God did begin to open up to me on more topics, but built upon the foundation of His love for Anne and me. This is the revelation both you and your wife need to hear from Him. Your wife has likely been cultivating this skill of hearing more clearly as she has worked through the reflection questions in this book. I'll cut to the chase – you need to catch up in this one area.

When Anne and I started to hear more clearly from Him, she would get paragraphs. I would get a few words. I wanted to give up. But I knew my future was with Him. I had to keep pressing in. You must do the same.

In Mirkwood forest, after Bilbo and the dwarves lost their way, a turning point for the company was when Bilbo climbed a tree to the top, above the forest canopy, to get the right perspective. Through hearing God more clearly, He will give you and your wife the right perspective. This is the help you need. Don't shrink back from climbing the tree to hear Him more clearly. His perspectives are irreplaceable.

Wrapping Up

As men, we want to fix things. So, let's honor that. Here is your assignment, your checklist if you will, to help you and your wife get through this together:

- Read Anne's chapter on "Grieving the Losses" to better understand the losses your wife is feeling.
- Consider and write down the losses you have felt. Write them somewhere in a manner you'll have them later.
- If you've tried to 'pull' your wife through grief, seek her forgiveness. If your wife has felt abandoned emotionally, seek her forgiveness. Ask God if there is anything else you need to apologize for in this season and then seek her forgiveness.
- Offer your availability to your wife for whatever she wants and needs from you. It may sound something like this:

  I realize I have not been everything I need to be for you in this season. I want that to change. I am committed to us both getting through this together. Please tell me, how can I best help you?

- If you have not yet done so, schedule a weekend away with your wife to be available to her; use this weekend to camp out in Mirkwood seeking God together. Reserve a vacation rental with multiple rooms so you can split up for alone time with God. Do not plan any extensive sight-seeing. Do not take any work with you. See the suggested schedule for the weekend away in Appendix 2.
- Re-read Chapter 4: "Gentle Whispers." Start practicing daily. Write down whatever you hear. Just 5 minutes a day will change your lives. Don't be a Naaman. (See 2 Kings 5:1-14 to refresh your memory of his story. In short, don't resist doing something simple that God can use to bring great healing.) Get started on this so that you can start hearing more clearly before your weekend away.
- Take your weekend away.

Finally, it has been said that after a trial, healing is pretty much complete when you can be genuinely thankful for all the good things God produced from that trial. The lasting good outshines the dark season of heartache. With that perspective, may this prayer be a guide for you as you bring all of this to God.

PRAYER:

Heavenly Father, the one who sees us and hurts with us in the midst of life's struggles, help me to recognize the losses I have experienced in this season. Help me to honestly grieve these losses with my wife and not attempt to simply bury them. Help me to lovingly tarry with my wife as she processes her grief so that she feels your love through my presence and that we emerge on the other side together. Guide us through this season of healing as we trust in you. You are good. Help us to discover the good that you will produce through all this. Amen.

REFLECTION:

What losses can I identify associated with our struggle with infertility?

____

____

____

____

God, what good are you producing in the midst of all this?

____

____

____

____

HEALING MEMORIES EXERCISES [6]

(You can do this alone between you and God,
but it's even better to do it with a friend who loves you.)

1. Ask God, "What is the root of me feeling
   unworthy?" (Write down what you "hear" in your
   heart or any memory that suddenly pops into your
   head. Don't argue with it.)
2. Write down the feelings you have associated with
   this memory/event.
3. Pray: "God, please take these feelings of (________)
   and come in and heal the wounds in my heart, soul
   and mind that are causing them. Let your healing
   oil pour deep into my heart, soul, and mind and
   bring healing and cleansing from all wounds."
4. Close your eyes and picture the event. Ask Jesus to
   show you where He was in that moment, and then
   look for him in the picture in your mind. See what

> He is doing or saying. Allow this memory to replace the old one.

5. Think about the event again and see if you still have negative feelings around the event. If so, repeat steps 2-3 and possibly 4.
6. Ask God, "Have I judged this other person or myself due to this event?" (Write down whatever is coming to your mind.)
7. Ask forgiveness for judging the other person or yourself, and release the judgment. Forgive the other person. Declare your freedom and cut off any consequences of the judgment.
8. Ask God, "Are there any lies that I am believing related to this?" (write down what you hear.)
9. Ask God, "What is the truth?" Then declare the truth out loud.

____

____

____

____

____

____

____

This appendix provides a suggested agenda for your weekend away to help process with each other and God your losses and grief, as discussed in the chapter, "For the Husband."

FRIDAY EVENING

- Drive and check in on the early side (e.g., 3 pm) to get settled before dinner. Do a simple dinner in-house (e.g., soup, take-out, delivery). After cleaning up:
- Dedicate the weekend to God in prayer. Invite Holy Spirit to do everything He wants to do to bring healing to your lives.
- Split up for an hour for personal prayer, Bible reading, worship, and reflection.
- Meet together for the remainder of the evening. Open her box of emotions. Start identifying each loss and the associated emotions that she feels. Write each one on a slip of paper. Let her take time

with each one. Discuss, cry, grieve together. There is no rush.

SATURDAY MORNING

- Simple breakfast in the vacation rental (brought with you).
- Split up for personal devotions (before or after breakfast).
- Meet together. Either continue her emotional box or start his box.
- Take a 30-minute walk outside before lunch to decompress.

SATURDAY MIDDAY

- Lunch – Simple in-house or easy in-town (minimal sight-seeing).
- Meet together. Pray/talk through any more emotions.
- Take a walk outside in the late afternoon to decompress. Decide on a nice restaurant for dinner.

SATURDAY EVENING

- Nice dinner out.
- Surrender Time (back at the rental) – Review each item that you wrote down to determine if you are ready to surrender the loss to Jesus.
- Collect those that are ready and destroy them together, as an offering of pain and trust to God.

Sunday Morning

- Simple breakfast in the vacation rental (brought with you).
- Split up for personal devotions (before or after breakfast).
- Meet together. Plan the next steps for healing and moving forward. This could include planning another weekend away, or scheduling nights to talk specifically on this topic. Listen for what God may be saying to you about next steps.
- Pack & checkout
- Sight-see in town.

Sunday Afternoon

- Lunch out
- Fun activity on the way home (e.g., hiking, shopping, etc.)

Notes

1. Mark Virkler, *How to Hear God's Voice* (Used with Permission – https://www.cwgministries.org/Four-Keys-to-Hearing-Gods-Voice.

2. The Passion Translation® is a registered trademark of Passion & Fire Ministries, Inc. Copyright © 2020 Passion & Fire Ministries, Inc. Used by permission. All rights reserved.

3. Joel Ansett, *It Takes a Long Time to Wait*, (*Layers*, 2023. The lyric and the original quote from the songwriter's son are used here with permission).

4. Graham Cooke, BrilliantPerspectives.com. Shared with permission.

5. *The Chosen*, Season 2, Episode 3 – find on YouTube.

6. Healing Exercises Used with permission from Chris and Jenie Nowak, Life Solutions, Course 1, www.freedom-4-life.com

www.ingramcontent.com/pod-product-compliance
Lightning Source LLC
Chambersburg PA
CBHW051510030726
47592CB00006B/2199